The Seán Mac Eoin Story

PADRAIC O'FARRELL

KU-188-002

THE MERCIER PRESS
DUBLIN and CORK

The Mercier Press Limited
4 Bridge Street, Cork
25 Lower Abbey Street, Dublin 1

© Padraic O'Farrell, 1981

ISBN 0 85342 664 3

To Noel

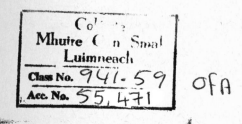
Printed by Litho Press Co., Midleton, Co. Cork.

Contents

Acknowledgements

I am deeply grateful to Seán Carthy, N.T., Ballinalee, for guiding me on an instructive tour of Mac Eoin country, for supplying information and for his scholarly examination of the first draft of the earlier chapters of my manuscript. While he pointed out errors and offered suggestions I take full responsibility for any discrepancies which might remain.

I thank Seán Mac Eoin's brother Jimmy along with his son Sean and daughter-in-law, Mary, for their help and hospitality. Thanks too to Sean's wife, Alice, his sister, Kathleen Trapp and nephew-in-law, Patrick Cooney, T.D.

I am indebted to many others for their assistance including Vincent Kelly, Editor of the *Longford Leader;* Nicholas Nally, Editor of the *Westmeath Examiner;* William and Edward O'Hanlon of the *Anglo-Celt;* the Director Alf Mac Lochlainn and Staff, National Library; The Librarian and Staff, Longford-Westmeath Library; An t-Uas Breandan Mac Goille Choille, Keeper, and Gabriel Gaynor, State Paper Office; Miss Kerry Holland and Staff, University College Dublin archives; Gerry L'Estrange, T.D.; Tom Brady and Mick Gormley, survivors of North Longford Column; Brendan O'Reilly, R.T.E.; Colonel John Kane; John Jessop; Michael McCoy; Captain Peter Young; Jim Martin; Lieutenant Colonel Seán Clancy; Terence de Vere White; Bill McKenna; Diarmuid Moore; Patrick Melvin, Librarian, Oireachtas Library; Colonel Michael N. Gill; Colonel A. T. Lawlor; Patrick Devlin and Seamus Hunt. I thank the Mulcahy Trust for permission to use transcripts from the Mulcahy Papers and Dr Cahal B. Daly, Bishop of Ardagh and Clonmacnois for permission to include part of his homily delivered at General Mac Eoin's funeral. My wife Maureen again assisted with proof-reading. I am indebted to her and to my family for their continuing tolerance.

Foreword

While researching my book *Who's Who in the Irish War of Independence 1916-1921* I accumulated a considerable amount of material on the major personalities involved — far more than was required for the pen pictures contained in that work. I noticed, however, that one charismatic figure emerged who had not been the subject of any biographical study. It was with some trepidation that I set about righting this omission for, in the absence of elaborate documentation, an objective appraisal of a soldier-politician can be a daunting task. I made my judgement in the light of circumstances suggested by research alone and completely secure from the influences of any political affiliations. The opinions offered in this short biography, therefore, are the results of examinations of the relevant material available and interviews with contemporaries of Lieutenant General Seán Mac Eoin. Coming from both sides of our history's tragic divide, some of these lauded 'The General', others criticised him. None despised him.

I had no close associations with the man, with his supporters or with his critics. I hope these factors have resulted in my presenting a fair and unbiased account of a leading figure in Ireland's struggle for Independence, her Civil War and the half century which followed it.

PADRAIC O'FARRELL

1. Beginnings

In April 1893 the ageing William Gladstone, during his fourth Prime Ministry avowed '. . . the Irish question is the curse of this House. It is the great and standing impediment to the effective performance of its duties.' On 1 September of that year Gladstone's Home Rule Bill passed its third reading in the House of Commons but it was rejected in the House of Lords a week later. In the country whose destiny was being cursed as well as being debated by an alien parliament other events were taking place, other *impediments* were spawning. Douglas Hyde was forming the Gaelic League. In the south of France, Maude Gonne was currying favour with Lucien Millevoye, a journalist-politician, in the hope that he would aid Ireland's cause. Yeats, George Russell, Lady Gregory and others were inspiring a new Ireland with their literary endeavours. The split in Parnell's party following the Kitty O'Shea case saw John Dillon emerging as the anti-Parnellite leader in association with Tim Healy.

Andrew McKeon was the blacksmith at Bunlahy, Co. Longford. His wife Kate Tracey had been born at nearby Ballinlough while Andrew hailed from the Hill of Molly near Aughnacliffe. Both were connected with nationalist movements. Kate's grand-uncle had escaped at the great Battle of Ballinamuck in 1798 by smearing blood across his face and feigning death. Large numbers were hanged around north Longford in the aftermath of Humbert's campaign and that area always remained alert to the national cause.

The first child of Kate and Andrew was born on 30 September and was christened John Joseph McKeon. Shortly after his birth the McKeons moved to a rented house and forge at Clooncoose, Ballinalee. Ballinalee

11

— the 'ford's mouth of the calves' — was not far from Bunlahy but the village forge there attracted a greater amount of business. There the rest of the McKeon's large family were born: Michael, Andrew, Jimmy, Lena, Mary, Peter, little Owen, who died of measles shortly after birth, and the youngest Kathleen.

Kate McKeon was in the house one day when Father O'Farrell, the parish priest of Clonbroney, reined in his fine horse and commenced a friendly chat with the housewife. In the course of the conversation she asked the priest to bless Seán and Michael, the two children present in the house at the time. The clergyman bade her get water from the river, with which he blessed the boys. He told Kate that neither boy would ever be harmed by either fire or water — even as he grew into manhood. Kate placed her faith in the priest's words and throughout her life she seldom showed fear for her boys.

John McKeon grew up like any normal Irish country boy. He played football in the village with other lads and in the field behind his home with his brothers. At about six years of age he started school with Master Michael Connolly. The teacher had a nephew, with whom John was later to become closely associated, named Seán Connolly.

An average student, John was soon to receive chastisements from his parents for bringing books to read in bed. Master Connolly, however, did not like John's habit of missing school. He often stayed at home to help his father, but when he did he insisted on doing some study in the evenings. Master Connolly warned that he would not allow John enter for a religious examination which was due if he missed any more schooldays. John did not like this for there was a friendly rivalry between the Connolly family and the McKeons and John wished to bring credit to his household. He did miss school again and he was forbidden to come on the day of the examination. Disobeying 'the Master' was unheard of then but on the day the diocesan examiner arrived John McKeon came to school, and took first place in the class. John also became very keen on the Irish language and began using the Irish version of his name, Seán Mac Eoin, as early as 1904.

His father's business was growing and he soon needed the constant help of his strong, sturdy son. At fifteen years of age Seán became an apprentice blacksmith in his father's forge and soon his sinewy arms became taut with muscle as he learned to hoop a cartwheel or ram a horse's hoof between his thighs and hold it steady as he burned the red-hot shoe into place while nailing it home. Jimmy had the job of replenishing the half-gallon container of porter kept in the corner of the forge for his father's cooling-off periods, blacksmithing being hot, tiring work.

Oft-times Seán was despatched with the family jennet and trap to attend to the needs of the horses at the big house of James Mackey Wilson, M.P. for North Longford, at Currygrane. This was the birthplace of Sir Henry Wilson, Chief of the Imperial General Staff who was later shot in London, an action not approved of by Mac Eoin. Seán also went on occasions to the Edgeworth estate in Kilshruley, owned by Thomas Edgeworth . As well as remembering a great literary family, he recalled what he had heard about the Abbé Edgeworth (the Abbé de Firmont). That cleric had attended Louis XVI of France on the guillotine in Paris.

For these services his father got the grazing of two cows on the Edgeworth estate. Seán never spoke ill of these landowners. He respected straight-forwardness and the right of an individual to hold a point of view contrary to his own.

His life was being moulded through rather unusual

friendships with three men much older than himself. Edward Killeen owned a mill which was later to become the property of Michael Mac Eoin and be known as Mac Eoin's Mill. Edward was a religious man and he walked the lanes and fields around Ballinalee tutoring his willing young student in a strict moral code and an undying religious faith. Seán Mac Eoin was a Lay Dominican. There was an unusually strong tradition of membership of this Third Order of St Dominic in Longford as a statue erected by its members in St Mel's Cathedral indicates. He served Mass and was faithful to his religious duties.

Another associate of Seán's was Joe Dowling, a veteran of many campaigns on foreign fields who filled Seán with great tales of gallant acts in gory battles and of the right to freedom which is the desert of every man.

Then there was the Fenian Thomas Kenny. Thomas had Ireland's dark history at his fingertips and her welfare in his heart. Daily he related the atrocities of the Famine to his intent young listener: Ireland's unsuccessful Rebellions, the 'Year of the French', Father Murphy, Robert Emmet, the Manchester Martyrs — Allen, Larkin and O'Brien — publicly hanged in 1867. Thomas would finish his chat by rendering a ballad written by T. D. Sullivan to commemorate that incident:

> 'God save Ireland,' said the heroes;
> 'God save Ireland,' said they all.
> 'Whether on the scaffold high
> Or the battlefield we die,
> Oh! What matter when for Erin dear we fall!'

The friendship of these older men towards Seán was reciprocated, and when a few years later Edward Killeen, who had no close relations, was dying Seán spent many hours keeping him company and looking after his needs.

By 1910 Seán was taking an active part in politics, becoming a member of the Clonbroney branch of the United Irish League. That organisation had been founded in 1898 by John Dillon and William O'Brien in an effort to heal the rift in the Irish Party. Mac Eoin was a delegate to the North Longford Executive, the representative for the area being the celebrated J. P. Farrell who had published two historical works on Longford's history and had founded a newspaper, the *Longford Leader*. But at this stage the fledgling revoluntionary had no intention of taking up arms, although he realised that he could not rule out that possibility.

He set out to educate himself, studying geography, shorthand and all he could of the Irish language. In 1912 the introduction of the Third Home Rule Bill in the House of Commons was preceded by a rally of Unionists and Orangemen numbering up to 100,000 at Balmoral, Belfast. Addressed by Bonar Law, it boasted the biggest Union Jack ever woven. In Bunlahy, Seán Mac Eoin joined the Gaelic League classes and became more resentful of things alien to the Irish tradition. Already he was showing signs of his ability to take a firm, even dogged stand on issues of principal. A sharp discernment and keen judgement began to show in his character. Not for him any captivity by the emotive swell of heady oratory. Of a disciplined, rural background he believed in hard work and had little sympathy for some of the popular urban sentiments being propounded by Jim Larkin and others. His enthusiastic industry was soon to stand him in good stead.

On 19 February 1913 Andrew McKeon died at the age of forty-nine. As he was laid to rest in Colmcille, Seán — just nineteen years old, not then considered a mature age — realised that the onus was on him to provide for the family. The youngest girl Kathleen, then only two years old, was to become his particular ward, and a great bond of affection developed between them. All the family were close, however, and evenings of song and dance had been a feature of their home life.

Now Seán set about fulfilling his responsibilities to his widowed mother and the seven other children. He was assisted by his brother Michael, ten shillings worth of coal and a large store of determination. He worked hard and long. Within a year of his father's death he was able to pay £200 for four acres of land beside the family home. Before the Great War broke out in 1914 he had bought Robert Brown's small thirty-five acre farm for £400. This was about a mile away on the Granard side of Ballinalee. It had a small house with byres and barns. He put his sister Lena and brothers Andrew and Jimmy into it. In later years these out-offices were to serve as places of detention for persons convicted by Sinn Féin courts when the homestead became known as 'The Prison'.

The exact time of Seán's joining the Irish Republican Brotherhood is unknown, for his loyalty to the oath of that organisation kept his lips sealed on its affairs. Towards the end of his life, indeed, he wrote his autobiography but held that his oath forbade its publication until after his death. In spite of his hard work in the forge, however, he was always willing to lay aside his sledge or hammer to discuss local and national affairs with the men and boys of the district who made his place of work a meeting-house. He also found time to continue his education, helped by a Miss Connifry who conducted classes for a small fee in an old thatched house. Soon the Blacksmith of Ballinalee became legal-minded, astute and well read. Seán was developing into a leader among the community, and was often approached for advice on land dealings, property sales, meadow auctions and other affairs of the countryman.

During the months following his father's death the Home Rule Bill was passed a second time in the House of Commons but was again defeated in the House of Lords. In August the great Dublin lock-out began and in September the Ulster Volunteer Force backed the establishment of a Provisional Government of Ulster. Soon the Irish Citizen Army was founded and the Irish Volunteers. The objects of the latter were:

(a) To secure and maintain the rights and liberties common to all the people of Ireland.
(b) To train, discipline, arm and equip a body of Volunteers to achieve this.
(c) To unite for the stated purpose, Irishmen of every creed, party and class.

Irish Republican Brotherhood members formed the nucleus of the movement. Members of Sinn Féin and the Gaelic League flocked to village halls where many ex-NCO's of the British Army drilled and instructed them in musketry and minor tactics.

In April 1914 the 'Ulster Gun-Running' armed the Ulster Volunteers with over 24,000 weapons and ample ammunition. No action was taken against them by the British government who had prohibited arms' importation. In July, 1,500 rifles and 40,000 rounds of ammunition were landed by Erskine Childers in the 'Howth Gun-Running'. In marked contrast, a vigorous attempt was made by the British authorities to seize them.

At Ballinalee, the local blacksmith became a twenty-year-old Section Commander in the Clonbroney Company. Soon he was a Lieutenant and later Company Captain. The only weapon available for training was a single German Mauser. Firing practices were carried out in Feeley's quarry and even young Jimmy Mac Eoin was given an occasional shot. His older brother Andy one day challanged him to a competition. They placed a matchbox on top of the shaft of a cart. The sworn-in

Volunteer missed but Jimmy hit the matchbox. Michael Mac Eoin was a Volunteer too.

Men of the land were soon to become familiar with the altogether unique scheme of military command and its plethora of regulations, instructions and circulars. A 'Scheme of Military Organisation of the Volunteers' issued on 16 December 1914 set down ranks and insignia. According to it, Seán Mac Eoin should have worn 'three trefoils and two dark green bands' on his cuff.

Volunteer leader John Redmond had caused a split in the movement by a speech at Woodenbridge, Co. Wicklow on 20 September 1914 when he advocated that they had a duty to join the British Army and fight 'wherever the fighting extends, in defence of right, freedom and religion, in this war'. Of about 180,000 Volunteers, over 12,000 rejected Redmond's policy. Eoin Mac Neill led this group, known as the Irish Volunteers as distinct from Redmond's National Volunteers. The minority's policy of allegiance to Ireland alone was endorsed by an October meeting at the Abbey Theatre which also established the force as an organisation for the defence of the nation and its unity, whose goal was the replacement of Dublin Castle rule with a national government. Although a minority, the movement embraced prominent figures, many of them influential members of the Irish Republican Brotherhood who had already decided on insurrection while England was at war.

An impassioned speech by Pádraic Pearse, a schoolteacher revolutionary, at the grave of the great Fenian Jeremiah O'Donovan Rossa roused national sentiment by its sheer oratorical power. Dressed in the uniform of the Irish Volunteers, his mighty waves of emotion broke on a receptive throng:

    . . . we know only one definition of freedom: it is

Tone's definition, it is Mitchel's definition, it is
Rossa's definition. . .

. . . splendid and holy causes are served by men who
are themselves splendid and holy. . .

. . . the fools, the fools, the fools, they have left us
our Fenian dead, and while Ireland holds these
graves Ireland unfree shall never be at peace. . .

Now little Kathleen Mac Eoin held a lantern for her
big brother as he shod horses during the dark evenings
and spoke a friendly word to all who called. Or she
might clamber into his huge arms by the fire at night
getting that protective feeling which most small children
receive from their father.

But Seán was more pensive now. Something was
happening up in Dublin. A Rebellion. A government of
Ireland had issued a Proclamation. The city was ablaze.
Snippets of news reached the sleepy village of Ballinalee
and Seán wondered how much of it was true. People of
the countryside were often apathetic towards national
aspirations; sometimes they were even cynical. The
Irish Parliamentary Party had served as a bulwark
against an inherent urge to achieve independence, a gut
inclination among earlier generations. The immediate
reactions to Pearse's oration at Rossa's grave had
receded and many now regarded his Rebellion as
blackguardism or, at best, misguided patriotism. Then
came England's blunder by adding to the graves of the
'Fenian dead.' The leaders of the Easter Week Rebellion were executed.

More manifestations of the change of mood throughout the country occurred in the midlands. Count
Plunkett, deported for his part in the Rebellion, was
elected to Parliament for North Roscommon in February 1917. Then a by-election in the Parliamentary
stronghold of Longford South became imminent. Mrs

Margaret Pearse, Mrs Clarke and Countess Plunkett descended upon the constituency in support of the imprisoned Sinn Féin candidate, Joe McGuinness, who awaited the result in Lewes Jail. Their electioneering slogan was *'Put him in to get him out'*. The result was delivered: McGuinness the loser by twelve votes. A recount brought a different result and Longford celebrated a thirty-nine vote win for McGuinness who refused to take his seat — even if he could. Seán Mac Eoin summed up the situation by saying:

> This change of mood was first reflected in the election of Count Plunkett, father of the executed Joseph Plunkett, and later of Joseph McGuinness, a convicted rebel 'felon' then serving time in Lewes Prison, as proper representatives of the Irish people in preference to candidates of the Irish Parliamentary Party.

The Irish Volunteers in Longford protected Sinn Féin voters at the polling booths during that by-election which was held on 9 May. McGuinness's campaigners had suffered severe harassment in Longford. There was a resurgence of interest in the movement, helped by visits to the area by people like Michael Collins, Frank Thornton and Thomas Ashe, who was arrested for a seditious speech delivered at Ballinalee.

There was a striking similarity between Mac Eoin and Michael Collins. Considerable physical proportions and strength, contempt of bureaucracy, commonsense and humanity were qualities which each possessed, and they became close friends. Seán described their first meeting in the forge: Collins asked him to take on certain tasks in Volunteer organisation and to command the local unit, implying that it would be a full-time occupation and that he would have to hire a man to carry on the work of smithy. As breadwinner and the sole supporter of a mother and a large family, that was a big undertaking.

'You must do it,' said Collins.

'I must not,' spat back Mac Eoin.

'You must.'

'I must not.' This time more emphatically he added, 'You'll have to be a better man than I am before I can agree to that.'

'But I am a better man than you,' replied Collins. This led to what Mac Eoin himself described as 'the struggle of two hefty young savages' but what the world knows to have been Michael Collins' favourite pastime — wrestling with friends. Seán admitted to his being beaten in the contest by a most effective method — Collins' roaring into his ear. Mac Eoin was later to say, 'In my opinion any country at a certain period in its hour of need has a figure emerge who fills the requirements of the time. I think that Collins was such a figure.'

Further protective duties during the 1918 election, when Sinn Féin won seventy-three of one hundred and five seats, bound the Volunteers closer together and part of North Longford was formed into a battalion area within Longford Brigade whose brigade commandant was Thomas Reddington, an itinerant woodwork instructor. The new battalion was commanded by Seán Mac Eoin. He had Seán Connolly as vice-commandant, Seán Duffy as adjutant and Frank Davis as quarter-master. Companies within the battalion area were located at Edgeworthstown (Mostrim), Killoe, Mullinalaughta, Drumlish, Ballinamuck, Colmcille, Dromard and Ballinalee. Later on Granard, Finea and Street replaced Drumlish, Dromard and Ballinamuck, and the unit was designated the First Battalion.

The Volunteers were gaining the respect and the support of the people and complaints were coming to them which previously had been reported to the RIC. Sinn Féin courts and arbitration boards were being availed of and their decisions accepted.

When the British House of Commons, by 301 votes to 103, extended conscription to Ireland Father Markey and Father Ratigan of Ballinalee joined with many other Irish clergymen in opposing it. A 'Pledge Sunday' was observed as a token of opposition and a national strike took place on the following Tuesday. Seán Mac Eoin closed his forge on that day and donned his best suit. He spent the day recruiting for the Volunteers and collected nearly a hundred names. Only a few turned up regularly for drilling but perhaps the use of only one rifle — the loan of the brigade commander's — for training purposes was a discouragement.

Seán Mac Eoin, however, had his own revolver which he had held on to when his licensed shotgun had been taken in by the RIC. He, Seán Connolly, Ned Cooney (the brother of his future wife who was also brigade quartermaster and the brigade adjutant) and James Flood planned to improve this situation. Along with Seán Treacy of Aughagreagh, Mac Eoin, Seamus Conway and Connolly carried out a raid on the house of a Miss Sheridan in Kilnaleck, Co. Cavan. They recovered a number of shotguns which had been impounded by the RIC. and were being closely guarded by them there.

Deeds like this, although not of great individual significance, strengthened the growing awareness that, for the first time since the 1800 Act of Union the Irish people had declared through the agency of the electoral franchise against the previously accepted constitutional system of representation in Britain's Parliament, a native government would not be without firm and potent backing from Ireland's young men and women.

Yet, Seán Mac Eoin was ill at ease about one incident. On the very day the First Dáil sat and adopted a provisional Constitution and Declaration of Independence, an ambush of gelignite carters and their RIC escort took place at Soloheadbeg, Co Tipperary. Two constables were shot dead by a party under the leadership of Dan Breen. Mac Eoin did not approve of the action although it won widespread acclaim throughout the Volunteer movement. Seán claimed that the standing orders covering raids for arms or equipment laid down that life was not to be taken except in self-defence or as a last resort. He approved of raiding military targets for arms, nonetheless. (His critics would point out that Miss Sheridan of Kilnaleck could hardly be deemed a military target.) But it was what he considered an unnecessary taking of human life that Mac Eoin decried: '. . . some old flat-footed policeman at the tail of a horse and cart with a load of gelignite stuck in the cart' was not a worthy target for the Volunteers.

The new situation imposed on the conscientious Blacksmith of Ballinalee another concern. He was head of the IRB in Ballinalee and he recognised the movement's president as the president of the new Republic. He watched with some anxiety when the Supreme Council of the movement handed over its executive offices and functions to Dáil Éireann. Mac Eoin always held the view that the IRB, the Citizen Army and the Volunteers combined formed the army of the new Republic. He was later to point out that the British government recognised it as such by negotiating a Truce with Commandant Ned Duggan on 11 July 1921 through another military man, General Nevil Macready. (See also Chapter 14)

This conviction, bolstered by the mandate received from the people, gave Seán Mac Eoin sufficient justification for his campaign against military and police in Longford during the following two years. He received his schooling for the task ahead behind bars in Sligo jail.

In November 1919 Mac Eoin resisted the efforts of two RIC members to apprehend him while pasting up a poster publicising the Dáil Loan and also prevented Sergeant Ryan, who was in charge, from removing the poster. Taken into custody at his forge the next day he was charged with obstructing the police in the course of their duty, conduct likely to lead to a breach of the peace, and other minor offences. The resident magistrate Jeffries called District Inspector Dan O'Keefe to give evidence of character. O'Keefe was a vital cog in Seán's intelligence service. His testimony inclined the magistrate towards binding Seán to the peace but a harangue from the accused defining his interpretation of what that involved and almost asserting his right to wage war caused the speedy passing of a two-month sentence.

Before his release on 28 December, Seán befriended other prominent Volunteer prisoners. These included Alec McCabe, Professor Tom O'Donnell, Jim Hunt and M. J. O'Mullane. Valuable information and insights into the workings of the movement in other areas were willingly passed on by them and enthusiastically absorbed by Seán. Furthermore, the associations gave him a certain standing upon his release and consolidated his position as a natural leader in the community.

2. Early Engagements

The popular designation 'Irish Republican Army' evolved about this time although the term was never suggested officially nor adopted by any deliberate policy. The force began to step up its campaign against the military and RIC, the latter considered legitimate targets because they were, in fact, an extension of the British armed forces. They acted as their intelligence agents in every village and town in the country and their barracks were defended like military posts. All were trained in the use of firearms and almost all of them were armed. Although Seán Mac Eoin disapproved of the killing of 'flat-footed policemen' his early engagements with his First Battalion were against their strongholds.

Drumlish was attacked on 6 January 1920 and in June Ballinamuck and Edgeworthstown were attacked. Mac Eoin, however, itched to strike at a military installation and so it was with great interest that he noticed a known deserter from the Lancers in Longford's Military Barracks Upper — the 'Top Barracks' — residing in the locality. With Seán Connolly he often chatted up this man who boldly promised that he would help the local IRA procure arms. His tardiness, however, became infuriating to both men and they eventually challenged him to do something constructive. He explained that soldiers returning to the barracks at night often identified themselves to the sentry in advance by whistling a certain tune. He promised to go through the motions of giving himself up to the sentry and allow a party of Mac Eoin's men to 'whistle' their way up near enough to overpower the sentry and seize the weapons which he guarded.

Mac Eoin, Duffy, Connolly and Conway carried out the raid. They bagged eight rifles and a little ammunition and made their getaway in Tom Brady's car. At Ballymahon on the following night Mac Eoin distributed the weapons to selected men and delivered a moving speech urging that they be used in a manner befitting soldiers of Ireland. The response to his words netted another ten rifles, about 600 rounds of ammunition, four revolvers, grenades, signalling pistols and assorted equipment that very night when Ballymahon RIC station's garrison was forced to surrender. Ten rifles and 1,000 rounds were seized at Arva Barracks in September.

At his court-martial the following year, Mac Eoin claimed that he commanded the Arva operation and that another man was wrongfully imprisoned for it. Many people believe this man to be Tommy Early, wanted by the RIC since a note found in the slain Contable Cooney's pocket later read: 'If I am shot, Early is the culprit.' Yet a member of the raiding party later testified to Seán Connolly's being in charge. Was this a case of poor communication or an effort by Seán to protect a colleague? Those who avidly claim that there was friction between Mac Eoin and Connolly would certainly discount the latter theory.

It was after the Arva operation that Seán Connolly was transferred to GHQ and then appointed organiser in the Roscommon area. Mac Eoin was appointed vice-commandant of the brigade in addition to his duties as commandant of the First Battalion. Seán Murphy of Granard replaced Connolly on the First Battalion staff. Seán Duffy was still adjutant and Frank Davis quartermaster. Mac Eoin's company commanders then were Hugh Hourican in Ballinalee, Seán Murphy (later Michael Mulligan) in Granard, Larry Kiernan in Mullinalaughta, M. F. Reynolds in Killoe, Pat Finnegan in Colmcille. Jim Killane led Rathowen and Street Sections while Finea Section had Harkins in charge.

In November, the North Longford Flying Column emerged. Its most regular members were Seán Mac Eoin, Seán Duffy, Seamus Conway, Mick Gormley, Jack Hughes, Tom Brady, John McDowell (the 'Bun'), Paddy Finegan, Mick Mulligan, Michael F. Reynolds, John Moore, Paddy Lynch, J. J. Brady, Larry Geraghty, Seán Sexton, Paddy Callaghan, Jim Sheerin, Mick Kenny, Pat Cooke, Hugh Hourican and James Farrelly.

There was a camaraderie among these men which might not be expected of a group engaged in guerrilla warfare. 'Nothing but fun and games' was how Jim Sheerin described their leisure-time antics. At ceili or barn dance, the men of the column were favourites with the ladies. Seán was as hearty and as full of the same *joie-de-vivre* as the best when it came to leaving aside the Luger for the lassie.

When Michael Collins came on military business the evenings invariably ended in a song, a joke, and a drink with some of the men of the Column. A word must be said in passing about other reasons for Michael Collins' visits to north Longford. His sweetheart was Kitty Kiernan, daughter of a Granard hotel proprietor. This establishment was soon to figure in Mac Eoin's operations. There are affirmations and denials of reports that an unwritten cease-fire existed whenever Collins came a-courting Kitty. Michael and Seán often met at the house of Eily Flood when the Big Fellow's courting was over. Musical evenings would be arranged to distract attention from the two big men who would retire upstairs for serious consultations. Collins and Mac Eoin, however, often ended their business quickly and joined in the sing-song organised to cover their movements.

3. Ballinalee

Michael Collins was still urging Seán Mac Eoin to employ a man to do his work in the forge so that he could devote his full energies to military duties. After all, there were records to be kept. Mac Eoin would have no part in the keeping of records, remarking that he was a fighter, not a writer. Erskine Childers was sent down to sort out the clerical mess but he departed in despair.

But Mac Eoin did eventually desert the forge. Indeed, the whole North Longford Column which evolved after 1 November went on the run. Mac Eoin's chief source of information, a Dungarvan born inspector of the RIC, was replaced by a man called Kelleher. This officer had a mandate to clean up the area and Collins sent instructions from GHQ that he and a Constable Cooney were to be executed. Some difference of opinion cropped up about the latter, a religous man who lived in the area and was respected by many.

But Mac Eoin's other sound contacts — the secretary of the Freemasons and the secretary of the British Legion in Longford — informed him of the imminence of a reign of terror and so he took action.

Both men were to have been shot on Hallowe'en but only Kelleher could be found that night. He was in the company of a bawdy band of drinking Black and Tans in Kiernan's Hotel, Granard, when he was lured to his doom.

Next morning, Mac Eoin's quartermaster Frank Davis carried out the second execution at Clonbroney on a by-road to France. The local parish priest, Father Markey, had some words with Seán about the removal of the constable's body. He also spoke to him when he returned some hours later for he had just been interrogated by police who broke into his home and buffeted

him, threatening violence. He dashed away as they were
supposedly planning a spot for his execution. Later that
day Father Markey's curate Father Montford brought
the news that the Crown forces planned to burn
Granard that night.

This was not surprising. Mac Eoin completed plans
for defending Ballinalee and left affairs in the capable
hands of Frank Davis. Then he hurried to assist Seán
Murphy, bringing some of the column on bicycles.
Murphy was second-in-command of the battalion and
had been posted to Granard in case the enemy struck
there first. At nine-thirty that evening a public house
disgorged a rampant, revenge-thirsty mob who began to
spill petrol or oil about a shop near Moxham Street. The
north Longford men opened fire and the Crown forces
were compelled to return to their barracks.

As Mac Eoin returned to Ballinalee early next morning, he realised that the village's position was now all the
more vulnerable. The enemy would be further enraged
at being thwarted in Granard and would strike at the
heart of north Longford's resistance with all their might.
It was a weary leader who retired to bed assured that
Ballinalee was prepared. He prayed for the village as it
awaited its Calvary.

While he slept, rumours kept arriving: 'McGuinness
of Longford had been draped in a Union Jack and
forced to march through town!' 'Tans were pouring into
the area from Athlone and Mullingar!' 'Longford's
Temperance Hall was burned!' He awoke to the final
announcement: 'They're coming to Ballinalee tonight.'

Villagers collected in the church for a Novena. Father
Montford addressed a hushed congregation , explaining
that their leader, Commandant Mac Eoin advised
against evacuation of the village although he himself dis-
agreed. When the service ended it was a sad Mac Eoin
who watched all but a few faithful families leave the

village. He sighed before going with his men to a nearby church yard where they received General Absolution. Then he went to his headquarters in Rose Cottage to conduct the defence of a near-deserted village. Had he a mandate for his actions? He reasoned with himself again: 'There is a constitutional basis for this struggle. In December 1918 the people of Ireland, by an overwhelming majority, elected an independent parliament. That parliament, the First Dáil, assembled in January 1919. What had previously been a revolutionary army then became the legitimate force, a force now at war with the Crown forces.'

A red glow in the sky announced that they had set Granard alight. At the crossroads in the village he was surrounded by his comrades: Seamus Conway, Seán Sexton, Tommy Early and Jimmy Mac Eoin, a loyal and trusted brother who stayed alongside Seán throughout many encounters. Seán Duffy led a party at a schoolhouse on the Granard road. Frank Davis was located on the Ballinamuck approach, commanding Paddy Callaghan and John McNally. Up at the Protestant church Hugh Hourican was in charge of a detachment while the Killoe Company were alerted to watch out for any forces arriving from Longford. The defence plan envisaged the Crown forces arriving from the Granard direction, being attacked by the Rose Cottage detachment and being closed in upon by the outlying parties.

The vigil took place during a dark night of incessant rain. It ended at 1 a.m. on 4 November 1920. Between seven and eleven British lorries trundled from the Granard direction. They turned unexpectedly onto the Ballinamuck road. The leading vehicle halted at Frank Davis' position; the rear one was still on the Granard road with its headlights shining into Rose Cottage. All outlying detachments were under orders not to open fire until Mac Eoin's section commenced hostilities. Davis, therefore, could not take action.

Mac Eoin later referred to what happened as an 'experience' but to bard, balladeer, *seanchaí*, schoolmaster or *spailpín* the Battle of Ballinalee was an event in Irish history that had as many versions as it had reporters. Even the British contributed to the confused folklore which has evolved from the incident. They claimed they were attacked by 500 ambushers.

The first shots were fired after Seán Mac Eoin had sent Seamus Conway out to pitch grenades into the trucks as the attackers alighted. A party of British approached the cottage and Mac Eoin waited until they were quite near. He opened fire just as Conway's grenades found their targets. Troops scattered from the convoy and soon the defenders came under machine gun fire for the first time in their lives — a frightening experience within the close and dark confines of the village. They replied as best they could with their meagre allotment of 100 rounds per man. Reckless fire from the British assisted them, however. They fired into their own men in the inky blackness. Little wonder they considered they were up against 500 men!

After about an hour of confused fighting during which some of the Protestant church detachment failed to close in, Seán Mac Eoin to quote himself, 'impudently called for surrender.' To his amazement, he was asked, in reply, for his conditions. He opted for unconditional surrender and the demand rang out with the ring of sledge upon anvil.

There was a period of consultation in the dark recesses of the village buildings. 'What if we don't surrender?' asked the enemy. And when Mac Eoin answered, 'Then it's a fight to the finish,' fire was re-opened.

But something was different. The intensity of the fire was waning. Engines came to life and the British lorries, without lights, began creeping through the dark street.

Tyres crunched on broken bottles, snugged into damp loaves of bread — remains of looted Granard goods. One by one they left and as the last one eased across the Camlin River a grey dawn arrived and smiled on Ballinalee — in spite of its gory streets. Though pockmarked with bullet holes, the village was intact. The lorries bearing the attackers away were lost in the network of roads to the north. They did not reach base until three o'clock in the afternoon. Their casualties were not announced but it is unlikely that they were as unscathed as the handful of men in Ballinalee who began discussing the event which was to become the favourite topic of conversation at midland hearths for many a long night afterwards.

Parts of the discussions were about some people who disappeared from the column the next day. They had appeared to deviate from Mac Eoin's plan and were reported to have fled to Scotland to escape his wrath and threat of court-martial. Yet many observers say they were perfectly justified in taking the action that they did. They came home again. They were not court-martialled. Three of them fought against Mac Eoin later in the Civil War.

It ought never be forgotten that the leaders in the War of Independence were in charge of their own neighbours and the Irish temperament was anything but compatible with discipline — especially military discipline administered by a kindred spirit. Mac Eoin had no code of Irish military law to support his authority. He had to deal with the normal petty breaches of discipline as well as the more serious ones. And he had to handle them as the local blacksmith turned commandant. The task was not an easy one.

4. Between Two Encounters

Rumour among villagers and secrecy from official sources were the aftermath of the Battle of Ballinalee. Casualties were not announced from the affray in which a 'single lorry escort for a Kildare Divisional Commissioner of the RIC' was waylaid 'by hundreds of rebels.' Mac Eoin prepared the defence of the village against inevitable reprisal attempts. Seán Connolly, realising that the North Longford Column would be virtually under siege, brought Bill O'Doherty and a number of Strokestown and South Roscommon Volunteers to assist. There was tension as a police patrol arrived to transport Constable Cooney's family and belongings away from Ballinalee. Apprehension was felt too as sections were deployed to deal with the attack suggested by thousands of lights over the surrounding countryside. The invading forces, however, were nought but a profusion of Will-o'-the Wisps, Jack-o'-Lanterns. This phenomenon, *ignis fatuus,* had been the cause of more missed heartbeats among Irish campaigners than the flak of the most modern of weapons.

Gentlemen of the press visited Rose Cottage and got a first hand account of the fight in Heraty's, an establishment which had remained open during the event. Michael Collins was later to advise Mac Eoin of a Scotland Yard detective being among the reporters. Mac Eoin slept in Father Montford's house where he overheard Bishop Hoare complaining about Constable Cooney's body being left so long unattended on the roadside after his shooting. Father Montford put up no defence and on the following Sunday the bishop condemned the Volunteers' actions in St Mel's Cathedral in Longford. Mac Eoin thought

33

this a peculiar attitude for a man who, as a young curate in Carrick-on-Shannon, had served a prison sentence during the Land War. He therefore went to Longford and explained to Dr Hoare that the Volunteers were serving a lawfully constituted government, elected by the Irish people. Mac Eoin never wavered from this line. He continued that he himself was an officer appointed by the Minister for Defence with the government's approval and the sanction of General Headquarters of the army. He gave the bishop a mild rebuke, saying that the Irish hierarchy had admitted the Volunteers' right to fight for their people's freedom.

Dr Hoare admitted to being enlightened by these remarks and even wished Mac Eoin success with his operations. He gave his blessing, for good measure.

Every student of Mac Eoin's life must become aware of what often appears to be a conflict between Seán's sometime ruthless behaviour and his deep religion. The cynic might be forgiven for suggesting that his frequent reception of the Sacraments may have been to allay guilt pangs about his activities. He often appeared to be attempting to convince himself that what he did was right and proper. He might well have modelled the popular caricature of the revolutionary with the rifle in one hand, the Rosary beads in the other. As a soldier, Seán Mac Eoin dealt with death and with weapons of death. Soldiers have often worried about the lawfulness of their profession in the eyes of God. Less thoughtful or less contemplative soldiers suffer little in this respect. But Seán Mac Eoin was a man of consideration, a man of deliberation, a man of reason. He wished to tease out the morality of his actions. A non-drinker, he could not lose his qualms in alcohol. Such a man of conscience had to be certain about the righteousness of his calling.

His bishop's understanding of the situation spurred

Mac Eoin to greater efforts. He commenced a perimeter defence of Ballinalee and began laying mines and occupying positions covering approaches to the village. While this work continued, however, the British descended on the village early in November and occupied a number of buildings there. The column was forced to dig up their mines in order to return to assess the position. The occupying forces had taken over Father Montford's house, the school and the house of Pat Farrell, which was soon fortified to act as their main stronghold. Mac Eoin moved his men again and made his popular bold call on the garrison to surrender. This was refused. A pincer attack was launched on Farrell's and covering fire given to Mac Eoin himself and Seán Duffy as they crawled and cut their way through barbed-wire entanglements to place a mine at the gable wall. The North Longford brigade had a better record of mining successes than many more prominent areas of operations. Farrell's gable collapsed when the mine was detonated.

Still the British held fast and a fatigued column withdrew to rest. On 9 November, more troops arrived from Longford, occupying more buildings. Duffy's house was fired, a curtain raiser for the invaders' sweetest moment when the house and forge of Ballinalee's intrepid blacksmith was burned. Even this symbolic victory didn't appease, and Heraty's, Hannigan's, Fox's and Early's were soon blazing. The arsonists left the village to burn the home of that other great leader Seán Connolly. Mac Eoin's men returned and dispersed a party of Black and Tans who were making a show of bravado at the top of the village. Soon flares coloured the sky as the Ballinalee garrison signalled for reinforcements.

Seán Mac Eoin's next moves may have been the forerunners of his political career for he forsook the gun to embark on a new plan. Exhorted to burn the home of

James Mackey Wilson, the resident of Currygrane House and M.P. for North Longford, he discarded the suggestion and went instead to see Wilson. He told him that Currygrane was to be burned but that it could be preserved if he contacted his brother, Sir Henry, who was Chief of the Imperial Staff and secured a cessation to the burnings of innocent people's homes. Next he approached Reverend H. J. Johnston, the Protestant rector who was acting as chaplain to the forces of occupation in Ballinalee. This man was also an officer in the Ulster Volunteers. He too was given a direction to use his influence to have the burnings stopped. He was also warned that Father Markey, now under sentence of death, was not to be harmed in any way but was to be given his freedom. Whatever treatment was meted out to the parish priest by the British — even if that was death — would be repeated in his own case by the IRA.

That night the column struck again, knocking out a search-light mounted above the school-house. Black and Tans and East Yorks in different locations were fired upon. Each thought the other was haphazard in its fire control and the Yorks withdrew to Longford at dawn complaining about the ineptitude of the 'Tans'. The IRA cleared Father Markey's furniture from his house in their absence and an involved attack was launched on the school-house when these Yorks occupied it on their return.

Meanwhile Mac Eoin was rallying the brigade and preparing an ambush for a particularly officious RIC divisional commissioner from Kildare whom he blamed for the Ballinalee burnings. In this his force's mining attempt was less impressive and the ambush at Ter-licken merely embroiled them in an unwanted fight for survival. When they disengaged they were fed by Cumann na mBan members in the out-offices of Lisglas-soch House. The out-offices were chosen, it has been said, because there was a smell of sulphur in the house itself. Sulphur fumes having connotations of a demonic presence, these men who took on the might of the Crown forces with abandon were not prepared to dine in a room which was suspect, according to the superstitions of the countryside that they loved and defended.

The ranks of Carson's militant unionists spread far beyond the borders of the province and a company of Ulster Volunteers existed in Ballinalee. David Kenny, son of a rent collector for the Wilsons and therefore a despised landlord's agent, was company captain. One of its officers was Second Lieutenant William Chartres.

There had been an involved dispute over land between Chartres' father and his uncle. At a Sinn Féin court, James Victory passed judgement ordering Barney Kilbride, engineer member of Mac Eoin's flying column, to survey the land and divide it between the brothers. The verdict displeased Second Lieutenant Chartres. He reported Kilbride and Victory to the authorities. Auxiliaries and Black and Tans arrested Barney as he was measuring out the farm.

An IRA court-martial passed the death sentence on Chartres who demanded prisoner-of-war treatment. The company's lieutenant, 'Pash' Elliot, had identified IRA homes to the Crown forces and he too received the sentence. The British Army discovered Chartre's body in Currygrane or Gorteen Lough some days later and the IRA were informed of their discovery. Elliot was shot by the IRA before being dumped in another lake, Listraghee Lough, since locally referred to as Gleann Seonín Lake. Mac Eoin was later to remark of the incidents: 'That finished the Ulster Volunteers.'

The peculiar situation now existed whereby day-time search and sweep operations were carried out by RIC and Black and Tans in order to capture Mac Eoin and his men. By night, however, they withdrew to their posts in the village and Mac Eoin and his column were free to meet their own friends in their own village. It is seldom realised by historians or others who speak of 'The Battle of Ballinalee' that there were a number of encounters in the tiny hamlet. There was a day-light attack mounted on 9 December which continued into the night before the Crown forces got a foothold. One covering party sufficed for the column's attack on Father Montford's house held by the East Yorks and its simultaneous assault on the school-house. Seán Mac Eoin showed great shrewdness in the deployment of his forces and in concentration of his resources to achieve maximum effect. His intelligence system reported a number of messages which passed through Longford post office. One of these indicated that Ballinalee's new visitors were claiming that a garrison of 1,000 would be needed to effectively defend the village's few houses against Mac Eoin's men. The other, through comparing business letters, revealed the only proven spy in Longford during the war.

Ballinalee's British garrison was uncomfortable. Occasional periods of levity, singing or playing cards were invariably cut short by the smash of a rifle bullet against a shutter — Mac Eoin's column reminding them that their position was precarious. Plans were going ahead to rout them from Ballinalee. The blacksmith was planning this strategy . His proposals did not include the incident that was to change his life.

The cottage of the Martin sisters, septuagenarian spinsters, stood alongside a narrow road a short distance from Ballinalee and only a few hundred yards from the farm in which Seán Mac Eoin had comfortably settled his mother and some of the family. At this time, the Martin cottage was used frequently for meetings between Seán and his mother, brothers or sisters and for meetings of the column. Martin's was one of the 'safe houses' which dotted the countryside, havens for men on the run where they could be assured of a bite to eat, a bed in which to sleep and — more important — a welcome. After Ballinalee Seán Mac Eoin had despatched his column under the command of Paddy Callaghan, to Aughagreagh about three miles from the village. He himself remained to observe enemy movements throughout the night of 7-8 January. After dark, however, he went to the cottage to write a letter for his mother. Mrs Mac Eoin was there with Seán's sisters Molly and Kathleen and his young fifteen-year-old brother Peter. With Seán were his bodyguards Jim Sheerin and Mick Gormley, a trained ex-soldier of the British Army.

A party of about eleven Black and Tans with RIC under the command of District Inspector McGrath, raided the Martin cottage. They screamed for Mac Eoin as they fired rounds into the walls of the cottage and terrorised the women. Seán made his getaway from the house which, however, was surrounded. He lay low. The occupants of the house were harshly interrogated and when they persisted in their claim that Seán was not in the house they were all placed under arrest.

Meanwhile Lena Mac Eoin was returning from the village to the cottage. She was called upon to halt by an RIC constable but, thinking it was Jim Sheerin, she told her hailer to be off with himself. He replied by firing his rifle over her head.

Jimmy Mac Eoin, Paddy Callaghan and John McDowell too were converging on Martin's cottage to meet Seán when they heard the shooting. They approached the house under cover but were powerless to do anything as the women and young Peter were now being hustled outside. Not wishing to embroil them in any firing Seán decided to make a dash for it. Firing into his would-be captors and tossing a hand grenade or bomb into their ranks he cleared a way for his escape. As Seán melted into the night to seek out his comrades the leader of the raiding party District Inspector McGrath lay dead outside the now stilled cottage where women fretted after their ordeal and angry men murmured vengeance.

Now Mac Eoin became a wanted man in earnest. His name was in *Hue and Cry*, the publication which briefed Crown forces on Ireland's wanted men. The charge against him was murder. The odds against him were high. He might just have kept clear of the Crown forces that sought him out had he laid low awhile. But lying low was not for the Blacksmith of Ballinalee. And glory was awaiting him down the road at Clonfin.

5. Clonfin

Seán Mac Eoin gently disputed the inscription on the memorial unveiled at the scene of his greatest triumph. He was vice-commandant of the Longford Brigade and commandant of its First Battalion when the Clonfin action took place. He was proud of the brigade and so would have preferred if testimony had been borne to it rather than to the flying column.

The new year of 1921 was ushered in by a further strengthening of the Longford garrison. As pointed out by Collins, this action constituted a tribute to the brigade. It encouraged Mac Eoin to redouble his aggression.

The County Infirmary on Battery Road was now occupied by a unit of Auxiliaries whose brief stipulated making the county a living hell for all its inhabitants, belligerent or otherwise. The Ninth Lancers still occupied the Top Barracks while the First Battalion East Yorks Regiment were stationed at the Lower Barracks, later called after Seán Connolly who had held Mac Eoin's appontment as vice-commandant of the brigade before beginning operations in Roscommon and Leitrim. All the main towns of the county had strong Black and Tan/RIC garrisons.

Mac Eoin decided that the newly arrived Auxiliaries should be attacked. He sounded his usual sources of information on troop movement and an ambush was planned at an ideal position overlooking the approach to Clonfin Bridge on the Ballinalee–Granard road. This stretch was dominated by a large ring fort which offered excellent cover and within which he established his command post. Much less secure was a position opposite which a mine detonating party operated.

This party was to blow up the first Lancia tender on the scene, thus blocking the remainder of the convoy which would immediately come under fire from the fort and other positions overlooking the road. Details were worked out; reconnaissance was made; the position was occupied. The North Longfordmen waited again.

An ass and cart bearing a pair of fowl merchants from Granard passed safely over the mine but not before the couple held a discussion on how the road surface had become disturbed. Scarcely were they out of sight when, shortly before three o'clock, the sound of approaching tenders was heard from the Granard direction — the most satisfactory one for the ambushers because the Auxiliaries would be past the fort before fire could be opened. The date was 2 February.

Banter and good spirits prevailed among the Auxiliaries, sitting in rows on their vehicles. They sportingly waved a tricolour which they had confiscated at Mac-Cormac's of Mullinalaughta as a climax to their lively day patrolling north Longford. As a result of a mishap on the rise ahead the exploder and the battery necessary to detonate the mine were knocked over in hurried anticipation of an opening to hostilities. Soon the error was corrected and the leading tender jack-knifed in the air from the perfectly timed explosion. Fire was opened from the ambushers' positions and was returned initially by the Lewis machine-gunner of a tender. He got off little more than a dozen rounds, however, when he was picked off by Jim Sheerin one of the alert mine-exploding party. Further attempts by the Auxiliaries to regain control of the gun were met by rifle-fire and they were forced to seek more secure cover in culverts and beneath Clonfin Bridge. They prepared to sit out the situation for they were expecting more troops along. Previous military service stood them well for they found positions inaccessible to the ambushers' fire.

As signs of a stalemate became apparent Seán Mac Eoin called on the Auxiliaries to surrender. They held fast. A section comprising Seán Duffy, Tom Brady and Mick Gormley moved down from the fort to the roadside from where they could re-engage the enemy. They succeeded in wounding the officer in charge, Lieutenant Commander D. J. Worthington-Craven. Formerly a naval officer, he had received the DSO and had been decorated by the government of the United States. He had served in the Dardanelles and had commanded a destroyer in 1918.

But as he lay seriously wounded in a Longford roadside culvert his troops had little option but to cease fire and await the anticipated savagery of an Irish retribution. It came as something of a surprise then when Ballinalee's blacksmith arrived on the scene, competently ordering first-aid for the wounded, marshalling prisoners, ordering them to load their dead on their vehicles. Then he approached the dying Craven. The lieutenant commander was so impressed by Mac Eoin's chivalrous behaviour that he warned Seán of approaching re-inforcements before he died.

Mac Eoin was instructing the survivors to bring their wounded and dead back to Longford even as Seán Duffy was exhorting him to hurry away with the captured Lewis gun, the eighteen rifles, the twenty revolvers, the ammunition, bandoliers and other equipment taken from the enemy. The column began to withdraw along the axis of the Camlin river to the marshy sanctuary around Ballinlough, Killeen, Clonfin Lough and farther north where they were familiar with every sheep-track and bog hole. Here they would be secure, billeted comfortably among their own people.

Seán Mac Eoin, Tom Brady and Seamus Conway were still on the road when the first of the Auxiliary re-inforcements arrived. Their presence caused the approaching enemy to halt and to make an estimate of the situation, possibly in consultation with the one Auxiliary who had escaped the earlier encounter. The delay benefited the column. It gave Seán Sexton time to dispose of the Lewis gun and carry on, laden down with other captured equipment. He dumped the gun in a bog hole. Others were able to obtain a head-start in their withdrawal.

They were soon followed by the tardy trio, now coming under Auxiliary fire. But the column's own re-inforcements were arriving too. The most important arrival of all, an Irish dusk, was now at hand. No British pursuer would attempt to penetrate a hostile Irish countryside by dark. A few sporadic shots were fired at the disappearing figures but the broad and swarthy Mac Eoin escaped. Clonfin was over.

Like most encounters of the period, the action at Clonfin challenges the most meticulous winnowing of folklore from fact. Ardent Mac Eoin supporters present it proudly as an example of chivalrous soldiering in the best traditions of military gallantry. They go as far as claiming that the leader's behaviour in the fight lent respectability to the Irish struggle in the eyes of foreigners and that his adherence to the most honour-able usages of war were cited by a future opponent, Seán T. Ó Ceallaigh, in his United States campaign for recognition of the Irish Republic.

He did not kill indiscriminately. He took prisoners

and treated the wounded. And it is onto this very point that Seán Mac Eoin's critics latch in presenting their case. 'He should have wiped them out like the IRA did in every other ambush,' they condemn. They follow up with claims that Seán Duffy should have been in charge at Clonfin; Mac Eoin's leadership was suspect; his consideration for the wounded was to the detriment of adequate supervision in the capture and removal of the precious Lewis gun.

But whatever the criticisms, Mac Eoin's Clonfin ambush remains the most significant action of the North Longford Column/Brigade. In gaining that distinction it also emerges as the midland's greatest contribution to the War of Independence. The Mac Eoin column, operating within or representing the brigade, was the most active unit outside the theatre of events in Munster. This action of theirs was one of a number which helped bring about the July Truce. Being the first engagement after the January 1921 meeting of Dáil Éireann it put into effect the directives of that assembly.

A man of prayer, Mac Eoin had prepared for the fight by going to Colmcille. There Father Luke Plunkett heard his confession and he served six o'clock Mass. One Auxiliary remarked to Mac Eoin after Clonfin: 'You are decent. Why do you shoot us down?'

The Blacksmith of Ballinalee answered with another question: 'Why don't you and your colleagues remain in England and we wouldn't be forced to shoot you down?'

6. Capture and Early Escape Bids

Instances of Mac Eoin's bravery are legion. He worked on 'cartwheel' mines in his forge, using axle-casings as moulds, and he regularly carried out personal tests of the finished products at considerable risk to himself. On one occasion, he and his column suspected sabotage in connection with detonators supplied — allegedly from GHQ — for an ambush at Terlicken. The concrete mines failed to go off when the exploder was operated. Frank Davis and James 'Nap' Farrelly came under fire from the ambushed troops but took cover. Mac Eoin ordered a withdrawal of the column to Lisglassoch, covering the operation by remaining behind with Seamus Conway and Davis, two more extremely brave men. Davis attempted to go and retrieve the precious exploding device for future use but Mac Eoin stopped him. Enemy fire was sweeping the area between them and the cottage where it was. Then Seán Mac Eoin strode across the field and returned with the exploder and portion of the wires trailing after him.

Some sources claim that it was to elaborate on the North Longford Column's mining successes that Seán was called to GHQ early in March 1921. The Clonfin explosion had been a classic. It is generally accepted, however, that Cathal Brugha invited or ordered him then to lead an expedition of twenty-two men to London. It later transpired that Frank Davis was also asked. Brugha's plan was to execute the entire British cabinet. Mac Eoin disapproved of the idea, adding that he, a man of the country, had difficulty finding his way around Dublin, let alone London. After some persuasion — for Brugha was impassioned with his spectacular plan — Seán agreed.

On meeting Michael Collins later Seán was taken
aback when the Big Fellow confessed to knowing
nothing whatsoever of the proposition. He told him not
to go to London but advised him to report the incident
to the chief-of-staff, Dick Mulcahy, and to return to
Longford immediately. In future references by Mac
Eoin himself and others there arose some inconsistency
about this affair. In the main the controversy centred
around terminology. Did Brugha 'invite' or 'order'?

In January 1964, Seán was to say that Brugha,
apparently without the knowledge of his chief-of-staff,
adjutant or director of intelligence, asked him to
volunteer for the assignment. He said this to Dick
Mulcahy and reminded Mulcahy that Collins cancelled
the order and told him to get back to Longford where he
had enough to do. Although he became more estranged
from Brugha, Seán regarded him as a sincere person.
His tolerance of other's points of view was again
evident.

On his return to Longford, Mac Eoin travelled by
train to Mullingar. The IRA battalion there were
alerted by GHQ and given instructions to stop the train
at the Hill-o'-Down where Seán would alight and escape
the cordon which would undoubtedly be around
Mullingar railway station. This was inevitable, for word
had reached Dublin Castle that the charismatic figure of
the resistance in the midlands was abroad in the city and
a great manhunt was put into operation to effect his
capture. He would hardly attempt to travel by train,
they thought, but all possibilities had to he taken into
consideration. Confirmation of his being aboard the
train was received by the authorities who informed the
district inspector of the RIC in Granard. He in turn
wired his counterpart in Longford. The party sent to
Mullingar station to await the arrival of the evening mail
included RIC Constable Quigley who was an agent for

Collins but who was helpless to do anything.

On the evening before, the officer commanding Mullingar Battalion, Michael McCoy, was arrested and detained. But instructions about stopping the train did reach the battalion and were not acted upon. It was a worried Seán Mac Eoin, therefore who noticed the black and white Hill-o'-Down and Killucan signs through his coach window without any indication of the train's slowing down. Through the darkness ahead he detected the lights of Mullingar. As the train eased itself into the station, dull platform lights picked out dark RIC uniforms and steel bands of military rifles.

'Smith of Aughnacliffe,' he told his interrogators, 'travelling to Edgeworthstown.' But a shrewd constable examined his hands and noticed the welts and blemishes, legacies of the wielding of sledge on anvil, of sparks from hammered hot iron, acquired in Ballinalee forge. Another sharp policeman remembered the fine figure of a man pointed out to him once, a long time before hostilities commenced, in Longford. He identified the captive positively. Handcuffs were snapped on. An overbearing group of RIC and troops fell in on either side of their prize. They marched him out of the railway station and up the incline towards the Green Bridge which carried the Ballymore and Longford roads across the canal and railway into the town.

On reaching the bridge, Mac Eoin suddenly swung out ferociously with his fists, felled some of his captors and startled all of them. He dashed towards a nearby gateway but he was shot and seriously wounded. Falling, he dragged himself into a dark, narrow laneway. He might have managed to shake off his pursuers had not a routine RIC patrol noticed him. He was set upon again, kicked and roughly handled before being hauled to the police barracks. Mick McCoy heard the scuffling outside his cell. Despite heavy loss of blood, the rough treatment he was receiving and being securely in the custody of armed Crown forces Seán Mac Eoin yet again lashed out with his handcuffed fists and toppled another constable. 'I was as strong as a horse then,' he later recalled.

Shortly afterwards, however, the local administrator, Father Joe Kelly, was called in to attend to the heavily bleeding and quickly weakning captive, shot through the lung, bruised and buffeted. A revolver was pressed to Seán's face as they jeered: 'Mac Eoin the murderer, we have you at last.'

The capture sparked off intense IRA activity. Collins tore at his hair and screamed that Seán must be rescued at all costs. On 7 March he wrote to Cork No 2 Brigade:

> You will have seen about our friend. It is simply disastrous. They seem to have sent a pack up to town to get him. Evidently they got information that he was here, and they appear to have drawn a cordon across the country against his return. . . There is many an aching heart for him in Longford these days. Cork will be fighting alone now. . .

That statement — 'Cork will be fighting alone now' — conveys Michael Collins' opinion of Mac Eoin's worth in the struggle.

The British too realised the importance of their captive. They hurriedly moved him to Wellington Barracks, then occupied by the First Battalion of the East Yorkshire Regiment under the command of Lieutenant Colonel T. A. Headlam. Their prisoner needed to be hospitalised but they could take no rash chances with the prize captive. There was only one other man whom they would have preferred to have in handcuffs, one even then planning his friend's rescue.

Collins was making demands on his men as never before. At least three ambushing parties were organised and deployed on the Mullingar–Dublin road as soon as information was received that Mac Eoin would be moved to hospital. Their instructions were clear and simple: 'Hold up the convoy escorting Mac Eoin to King George V Hospital and rescue the Blacksmith of Ballinalee.' The main road to Dublin was covered as was the Killucan–Ballivor route, but the convoy made a detour towards Longford and across to Trim, thus never clearing the 'Dublin Bridge' out of Mullingar where scouts watched for its departure.

By coincidence, it passed close to Clonhugh where some of the Longford Brigade, including Seán's brother Jimmy, were resting. The faithful Paddy Callaghan led a party of approximately fifteen loyal followers. They lingered in the fashion of a wolf-pack deprived of their leader, close to where their column commander lay fettered. They contemplated a rescue attempt of their own volition, but what chance would they have against the might of an occupied military barracks? They were enthusiastic but despairing, at a loss for inspiration. Trucks and ambulance passed through the night. Beside the patient sat a British officer, his finger on the trigger of his sidearm. Perhaps fate was playing a part by the foiling of rescue-bids, for it seems likely that the officer had orders to shoot his injured captive rather than have him rescued.

In King George V Hospital (now St Bricin's) Seán met General Sir Nevil Macready, chief of the British forces in Ireland up to the previous year, for the first time. That officer was later to remark that Mac Eoin and Collins were two of the few people with a sense of humour with whom he had met during his period in Ireland. When Mac Eoin heard to whom he was speaking he remarked to Macready, 'You have a good job if you mind it.'

The hospital operating theatre came alive. Mac Eoin

needed surgery to have a bullet removed. Nurses prepared; surgeons scrubbed up; the anaesthetist stood by.
Then tension! The patient was refusing a general
anaesthetic. Seán had observed post-operative interro-
gation of ex-British soldiers on the IRA shot by Auxiliaries, coming out of anaesthesia. Questioned by an intelligence officer, they had responded in their stupor
and freely passed on vital information. That would not,
could not, happen to him. After all, he had information
which would be of enormous value to enemy intelligence: the houses used by Collins and his agents;
Longford's brigade structure and locations used for bil-
leting the flying column; the procedures adopted by the
IRA headquarters; IRB secrets (which he was to keep
till his death).

'A local only — and that's final.' So the operation
began with Seán in full possession of his faculties; in
pain but at peace with himself. His life was saved but his
health was ever afterwards affected; his wife was later to
state that bullet fragments had remained in his lung
causing serious respiratory complications.

His first visit to this hospital was to be repeated many
times when it was staffed by the medical corps of a
native army under a native government.

While recovering after his operation, Seán had a
number of visitors. Posing as his girl friend, there was
Brigid Lyons who had already met him in the house of
her aunt Kate McGuinness during his visit to Dublin and
to Cathal Brugha. Her uncle was Joe McGuinness, that
Sinn Féin candidate elected while still a prisoner. Her
ploy for passing information was to act coyly and
request the warder to turn his back as she bade the
prisoner farewell. Then she would slip Mac Eoin a note.
Nancy Killeen and Mary Brady also visited him.

Then there was a strange priest who commenced his
meeting by upbraiding Seán for his Volunteer member-

ship. Ever respectful towards the clergy, Seán endured the harangue. He had as much as he could take, however, and was about to cut loose with his tongue when the guards left the ward and his guest's face broke into a smile. He told Seán he was from the Big Fellow. An escape attempt had been planned. He would be moved from hospital the next day by a party of 'British troops' — Collins' men in disguise. Seán was given a time to be ready and a parting blessing that may have lacked canonical authenticity but was nonetheless sincere.

Fearing his progress might occasion a premature release he pinched his wound that night in order to sustain the inflammation. Next evening Seán got excited as the arranged time approached. About three hours to go! But what was this? British troops? Had he mistaken the time? Those faces — not like any Volunteers he knew. Not even like Irish faces. They were genuine British soldiers. By an amazing coincidence the plan for Mac Eoin's rescue had been timed for a few hours after his actual transfer to Mountjoy Jail had been arranged by the British authorities. Another transfer brought a crack warder, a native of Athlone, from an English jail to increase security for Seán's admission to Mountjoy.

Disappointed but undaunted, Collins tried again. A hack-saw, a can of oil, a bar of soap, a watch and a plan of the prison upon which was marked his escape route — all these items were smuggled into his cell by a lady doctor who was attending him. The saw was for cutting the bars of his cell window, the soap to fill the cut as it progressed, so as to prevent its discovery. The planned route from his ground-floor cell led to the exercise yard and beyond. A sentry would be distracted by a sympathetic warder, allowing Mac Eoin access to a wicket gate where a bicycle would be provided for him by a member of Dublin Brigade. Others would lead him to the house of Collins' close associate, Batt O'Connor, in

Donnybrook. Ironically, a visiting permit granted to Alice Cooney delayed the meeting with an envoy from Collins bearing details of the plan.

All night Seán hacked away at the bars. A little sawing, a hurried filling with soap when the sentry passed. The hard and furious work affected him in his run-down state. Next morning the prison doctor noted his high temperature and recommended that he be moved to a higher, more airy cell on the third floor of the jail.

Mac Eoin protested that he was comfortable where he was! He liked the ground floor. His mother was coming to visit him and would not be able to climb to the third storey. But the doctor's consideration for the sick prevailed and another rescue bid was foiled.

7. Rescue Attempt and Trial

Throughout Seán Mac Eoin's imprisonment in the King George V Hospital and Mountjoy plans for his escape were being discussed in the Abbey Street headquarters of the IRA. Michael Collins made use of reports received from Seán through his constant visitor Brigid Lyons, later Brigid Lyons-Thornton. This lady was to have the distinction of being the first woman commissioned in the National Army. Indeed, she witnessed the taking over from the British of the same King George V Hospital, now St Bricin's Military Hospital. She was then a doctor in the army's new medical corps and wore a uniform although refused a uniform allowance.

Another visitor, as already noted, was Alice Cooney. She had admired Seán from afar during banquets in Longford when her parents would entertain friends actively sympathetic to the revolutionary mood which prevailed at the time. She heard demands on Seán to speak at a public function and approved his reply that he wanted fighting and not talking. Cumann na mBan member, Alice and her sister Molly, with brothers John, Edward, and Mark, were involved in Longford's struggle, and Alice was bringing a message from Edward (Ned) to Seán in Mountjoy during that first real meeting of the future husband and wife.

Early in May a final decision was made in Abbey Street and the plan decided upon for a bold and daring escape attempt.

Dublin City Abattoir, off an avenue called after the old Blackhorse Inn, stood within hailing distance of Marlborough Cavalry Barracks, a fine example of adventurous high Victoriana dating from 1889. A feature of the striking building was its bright red minars, turrets and dormer windows. Before that first week of summer had ended, an early morning raising of a blind in a less ornamented upper storey window of a North Circular Road house was the signal which would cause consternation within the impressive barracks up the avenue. That house was occupied by the supervisor of the slaughter yard who also supervised the Fingal Brigade of the IRA. The signal by Charlie Dalton watching from an upstairs room, meant that the crew of a British armoured car within the walls of the abattoir (calling to escort supplies of meat to the barracks) had left their vehicle unattended.

Figures moved towards the slaughter yard. Paddy Daly, from a commanding position at the top of Aughrim Street, nodded to Pat McCrea, Tom Keogh, John Claffey and Peter Gough. The select men of the 'Squad' reacted. They strode into the abattoir and approached the car. Its driver returned but was immediately disarmed. He was made to swing-start the car for the raiders.

McCrea took the wheel as some shooting commenced, for the British crew were now alerted. The commandeering party leaped on board and the heavy 'Peerless' vehicle rumbled out of the abattoir leaving two British soldiers dead.

At Hanlon's corner there appeared to be two British officers awaiting the now slowing car. These were not British officers, however, but Emmet Dalton in the uniform he had worn while serving in the British army and Joe Leonard. They jumped into the car as it passed and away sped the daring party towards Mountjoy Jail.

A group of Collins' men and some women, posing as relatives of inmates demanding to see their loved ones, hurled abuse at the approaching 'British' in their mighty armoured vehicle. Sentries looked furtively at the protestors across the forged documents presented by the

car commander. Then, to clicking heels, the party were
admitted and Dalton and Leonard dismounted to enter
the prison block. They had another forged document
authorising the release of the prisoner Mac Eoin to their
custody.

The same prisoner was frustrated. On previous morn-
ings he had complied with smuggled instructions and
was in the governor's office with a complaint at ten
o'clock. This morning his warder's duty-roster had
changed and his visit was delayed.

At the vital hour Dalton and Leonard entered the
governor's office. They found not Mac Eoin, but six
warders with the governor. They bound and gagged all
seven. Over a hundred soldiers and Auxiliaries manned
their posts outside, unaware of what was taking place.
There were extra forces in the jail that morning, Auxiliaries from Inistiogue, Co Kilkenny. Officiously, they
set about recording all prisoners' finger prints. There
are many accounts of what took place in the governor's
office including one saying the release was thwarted
because of the governor's fearing the 'escort' would
execute their prisoner. Leonard himself, not long
released from the prison, was recognised by a warder
who was more than a little mesmerised at seeing him in a
British officer's uniform.

Meanwhile the plan whereby the 'visitors' outside the
gates were to harass the sentry in order to effect the
escape of the car was going awry. Shooting commenced.
This combination of misfortunes forced Dalton and
Leonard to withdraw without their prize. They re-
emerged, shooting their way out of the prison block.

That the raiding party escaped unharmed was a major
feat in itself, and as the unpursued 'Peerless' dashed out
to Clontarf its occupants became hotter as the engine
overheated. It was also a heated Michael Collins who
received news of the failed rescue bid for he had

promised Seán Mac Eoin's mother that his next visit to her would be in her son's company. He appreciated the daring attempt, however, and wrote in glowing terms to the adjutant of the Longford Brigade some days afterwards: 'The men worked gloriously and gallantly, but they just failed to achieve complete triumph. It was nobody's fault. There was no mistake made. Things went on splendidly up to the last moment and then there was a mishap.'

Outside the prison significant events were taking place. The Better Government of Ireland Act had become a reality and on 19 May the first Catholic Viceroy of Ireland, James Talbot — Lord FitzAlan — was appointed to office. 'He won't have many Catholic calling-cards,' was the cynical response to this move, considered by the British government as a grand gesture of conciliation.

The 'Partition Elections' were called for northern Ireland and southern Ireland. On 19 May the twenty-six county election was held to select 128 members to a southern Ireland 'House of Commons', thirty-three of whom would be entitled to sit at Westminster. Sinn Féin, however, regarded the polling as a selection of deputies for the Second Dáil, all of whom would take their seats in that assembly on subscribing to the Republican oath. Their candidates were returned unopposed, making a farce of the Partition Bill. In the company of Mrs Margaret Pearse, Countess Markievicz and other distinguished personalities of the struggle for independence, Seán Mac Eoin was elected for his native Athlone –Longford constituency. He was thereby foisted into politics, a career in which he was not always to be happy. He faced his trial, therefore as a representative of his own people.

For his incarcerated friend nothing was beyond the bounds of possibility and right up to Seán's trial Michael

Collins was contemplating other plans to seize prosecution witnesses and to smuggle into Mac Eoin through his solicitor Michael Noyek revolvers to shoot his way out of the court room in Dublin's City Hall. But realism overcame adventure and on 14 June Mac Eoin faced his accusers.

A getaway car was waiting outside in hope and his two guards were smaller than he. Seán considered trying to take the rifle from one and to force his way out using the other as a hostage and cushion for the barbed wire entanglements outside. In his pocket he had two notes on bits of a cigarette box. One read, 'Trust in God. Have patience and wait.' The other said, 'Trust in God. Go ahead and do your best.' When his handcuffs were removed to allow him to make notes, he reached into his pocket, drew out the former and so made no move.

The charge read was 'That he did at Kilshruley murder District Inspector Thomas McGrath'. Mac Eoin's plea was 'Not guilty'. He said, 'As a soldier of the Irish Republican Army I have committed no offence either in National or International Law.'

A peculiarity of the prosecution's case was that there was no medical evidence to actually certify the cause of McGrath's death. Dr J. F. Keenan had been called to the scene of the shooting and had examined McGrath by the light of a bicycle lamp. He had noticed two small wounds in the neck, but there had been no inquest and no post-mortem.

Counsel for the defence could call no witnesses to the shooting as they too were all wanted men. Mr Charles Bewley produced character witnesses later in the proceedings. Maddox, Smith and Willford, Auxiliaries captured by Seán at Clonfin, testified that they had received due prisoner-of-war treatment from him and that he had given medical attention to wounded captives. It had little effect.

Like Emmet, like Pearse, he had his Speech from the Dock prepared. The following is a condensed version taken from an illuminated scroll which became a proud possession of his brother Jimmy.

At the opening of the court this morning I told you that I am an officer of the Irish Army and as such I claimed the treatment of an officer. But you are not here to try me as an officer. You are here to try me as a murderer — and why? Because I took up arms in the defence of my native land. Now, defence of one's land has ever been the privilege of the peoples of all nations and all nations have at times demanded the service of their sons in their defence as a right. I take my stand on that principle which has been fully approved by the people of Ireland and I am glad to feel that in carrying out my duty to my country I have always acted in accordance with the usages of war. The acts committed by me and by the officers under me could stand any test by any impartial tribunal. The prisoners who have fallen into my hands have been treated in a fair way. The wounded have been treated by us to the best of our ability. Some of these prisoners are being asked to bear witness to that fact — not that any punishment which the court intends to inflict should be mitigated, but just to show that my words are true.

The treatment which has been meted out to our prisoners and the wounded of the Crown forces has been different from the treatment which I received when I was wounded in Mullingar. There I broke away from the police. I do not deny that. Many of them were knocked down. They opened fire on me and the fortunes of war were all against me. I was struck down and afterwards, on the way to the barracks I was beaten with rifles. I was called a murderer in the day-room of the barrack in Mullingar. It may very well be understood what a hubbub there was when it was said in my presence 'Mac Eoin. the murderer, is in.'

I had only a few hours before called at the cottage near Ballinalee when it was surrounded by Crown forces — what I call alien forces. Two very old ladies were in the house. Naturally, it would not be feasible or right for me to start a row inside, I rushed out on the street and I met the forces, even though the odds were heavily against me. The District Inspector had a revolver, the other ranks had rifles at the ready. Fire was opened simultaneously by both sides. After the first exchange I noticed that the officer had fallen. His men were running away down the road. All I wish to emphasise is the fact that I fired at enemy forces, not at any particular person. I fired at them as they appeared before me. Two sergeants have sworn that they fired at me. The officer was between these men and me, and it was as reasonable to suppose that the officer was killed by one of them as by me. He simply fell in the fight. As to the allegations of police officers that I made statements at Mullingar, I do not know whether I did or not. Of one statement I have an absolute recollection, that is that a man from Ballinalee has been wrongfully convicted, even according to English law. It was I who commanded the attack and capture of an enemy post a Arva and not that man who has been imprisoned for it. Yet that man is suffering a long term of imprisonment for an act which he did not commit.

I am not guilty of the foul offence of murder and the people of Longford who have elected me their deputy in Dáil Éireann and the men and the officers with me believe and know that. They have full confidence in me, and I take this opportunity of thanking the people of Longford for their confidence in me. That confidence is my justification, as it was my authority for what I have done.

I wish to pay tribute to the gallantry and loyalty of the comrades who fought by my side. They have stood up to superior numbers and equipment, and they have come out victorious. From you I crave no mercy. As an officer of the Irish Army I claim the same right as I would be prepared to give you if you fell into my hands.

If you do not give me that right and if you execute me then there is one request that I make. It is, that you give my dead body to my relatives, so that my remains may be laid to rest amongst my own people.

Proceedings were brisk that day. The court closed to consider its findings at 3.55 pm. It re-opened to announce its verdict at 4.10: Guilty. At 4.12 it closed to consider its sentence. The passing of the death sentence on Mac Eoin brought widespread sympathy — including that of the late Inspector McGrath's relatives.

There have been allegations that the British Army sent a secret message to the Longford Brigade asking them to hand in their weapons in exchange for Mac Eoin's release. Seán sent an order down to his comrades, forbidding any compliance with the offer.

The Blacksmith of Ballinalee would await the fate suggested by a torn cigarette package. Fate would appear to have played a significant part in all the Mac Eoin rescue bids although the coincidences connected with them have not gone unnoticed by some speculators. They refuse to accept that mere chance brought about his transfer to Mountjoy immediately before the hospital rescue bid. Neither are they unquestioning about his abrupt move to the prison's third floor on medical grounds before another attempt. They also like to ask why the company of Auxiliary re-inforcements arrived from Kilkenny on the morning of the armoured-car rescue bid and, more pointedly, why the same car was not pursued out to Clontarf.

Their explaination is sensational and implies that the mighty Collins intelligence system was hoodwinked by a single prominent double-agent.

8. Release

On 25 May 1921 an incident which had been contemplated for over a year finally took place. In the most extensive operation of its kind mounted by the IRA, Dublin's Custom House was burned. In broad daylight the building was raided, its staff banded together and held while a party rushed through corridors spilling petrol and paraffin oil. The occupants were then released and instructed to rush to safety while the magnificent Gandon edifice with its impressively defined Palladianism and fine Portland stone face was fired. Its flames proved to be a beacon in the darkness of Ireland's tragedy for they were fuelled by documents and records of Inland Revenue, Estate Duties, Local Government, Stamp and Assay Offices. Thus they symbolised the final collapse of British civil administration in Ireland. This great gesture of defiance in the face of a terror campaign has since caused historians heartbreak by its destruction of vital information but it brought peace feelers from the British government.

Lord Derby was seen at the Gresham Hotel. He contacted Cardinal Logue and arranged a meeting with Eamon de Valera. Sir James Craig came too — some say to offer De Valera the prime ministry of a United Ireland with ribbons, if not strings attached! The support of the Boer commander Jan Christian Smuts, South African prime minister, was solicited by Roger Casement's brother Thomas. King George V was about to visit Ireland for the opening of the First Northern Parliament whose prime minister, Craig, had sent an invitation to Sir Henry Wilson, chief of the Imperial Guard, to attend. Wilson declined on the grounds that he might shortly be pouring thousands of troops into Ireland to finally crush its Rebellion. Despite his warmongering words, truce negotiations continued as Wilson's fellow Longfordian languished in Mountjoy Jail.

Seán Mac Eoin was an inspiration to his fellow-prisoners and at least one of them was moved to poetic endeavour in praise of him. Two men, Richard McGough and Jim Hunt, were serving sentences for taking control of a train from Kilfree Junction in south Sligo to aid an attack on Ballaghadareen RIC Barracks. They had never served under Mac Eoin but the spontaneous admiration for the Blacksmith of Ballinalee is expressed by a simple verse written by McGough in Hunt's personal diary dated as late as 11 January 1922:

'Long may you live, Leinster's hero,'
Is a nation's prayer for thee;
You are Ireland's pride and glory,
Seán McKeon of Ballinalee.

The Truce was agreed to on 9 July and it came into effect on 11 July 1921. Three days later Seán Mac Eoin had a surprise. Still in the condemned cell he awaited another visit from Brigid Lyons. She arrived, accompanied by a man introduced by the warder as a Mr Grey. The warder withdrew and the Blacksmith extended a hearty welcome to the Big Fellow.

The Truce was received with enthusiasm by many, with reservations by a few. Normality had returned, it appeared. A victory had perhaps been won — but not everybody was convinced. Tricolours were flown. Young Volunteers claimed prizes of victory from their womenfolk and drank heady liquor to give vent to their patriotic rendering of *Amhran na bFiann*.

Older men silenced them and declared that the Truce was but a ceasefire, not a solution. Wasn't Collins still touring the countryside interviewing battalion and company commanders while reorganising his intelligence system? Weren't there rumours that he was about to import vast quantities of arms? Weren't the British consolidating and preparing for further hostilities? Building concentration camps, some vowed!

Violations of the Truce were frowned upon by leaders on both sides. This was a delicate situation. Negotiations were imminent. Free and frank discussions were desirable, therefore all elected representatives held in prison were released; all except Seán Mac Eoin. Dublin Castle made the announcement on 6 August:

> In keeping with the public undertaking given by the Prime Minister that His Majesty's Government would facilitate in every practicable way the steps now being taken to promote peace in Ireland, it has been decided to release forthwith, and without conditions, all members of Dáil Éireann who are at present interned, or who are undergoing sentence of penal servitude or imprisonment, to enable them to attend a meeting of Dáil Éireann, which has been summoned for 16 August.
>
> His Majesty's Government have decided that one member, J. J. McKeown, who has been convicted of murder, cannot be released.

Michael Collins was furious. He drafted a reply for Eamon de Valera to deliver which was little short of an ultimatum:

> There can, and will be, no meeting of Dáil Éireann unless and until Commandant Seán Mac Keon is released. The refusal to release him appears to indicate a desire on the part of the English Government to terminate the Truce.

Allegations have been made suggesting the president's reluctance to accept Collins' draft but Eamon de Valera's announcement to the British government disclaimed responsibility for proceeding further with Truce negotiations and included a further tribute to Mac Eoin. It read, in part:

> The whole Irish people are proud of him for in him they see the patriot soldier that their history has taught them to love. He is the ideal citizen whose dauntless courage and readiness to sacrifice himself for his country is matched only in his chivalry as a soldier. We, the Irish Government and the Headquarters Staff of the Irish Army are proud of him as a splendid representative of the type of Irish soldier this fight has developed and as a living model of what we want our army officers to be. His conduct in the field as borne testimony to at the British court-martial and his speech and conduct at the trial itself proves to the whole world the manner of men he is. In British legal phraseology he is termed a murderer; but for us, and I believe for the world, he is a heroic Irishman.

The British cabinet were reluctant to concede but they contacted Lloyd George in Paris. He is alleged to have been playing with a grandchild when the vital question was brought to him for decision. Anxious to get on with the game with grandfather, the child is supposed to have said, 'Oh can't you let the man live and come on and finish our game.' General Macready's view was that the government had already parleyed with men who had committed crimes as grievous as Mac Eoin's. Was his lenient attitude influenced perhaps by his earlier hospital-ward banter with Mac Eoin? Or by the fact that De Valera had recently been captured by accident at Blackrock and immediately released? He held that if the government 'could recede with dignity from the position taken up' it would do well to release Mac Eoin. The attorney general, Sir Gordon Hewart,

remarked, 'We have swallowed the camel of negotiations with instigators and procurers and must not
wreck settlement by straining at the gnat of one more
release.'

There were discussions in Dublin too — and controversy. The government were not by any means unanimous in their support for the ultimatum. Michael Collins
and Eamonn Duggan went to the office of the *Irish
Times* with statements saying that unless Mac Eoin were
freed there would be no further Truce negotiating. Two
other members of the cabinet went along next day
refuting this. The same member of the *Irish Times* staff,
Hugh Curran accepted both statements. Many years
later Ruaidri Brugha was at pains to point out that it was
not his father, Cathal 'who seemed to oppose De
Valera's proposal to inform the British that negotiations
could not continue unless Seán Mac Eoin was released.'

On 9 August the *Irish Times* reported:

In the *Irish Times* of Monday we printed the
following paragraph:
'It was officially stated last night on behalf of Dáil
Éireann that there can be and will be no meeting of
Dáil Éireann until Commandant J. J. McKeon is released. It was added that the refusal to release him
appears to indicate a desire on the part of the English
government to terminate the Truce.'

Mr Erskine Childers, a member of Dáil Éireann
Publicity Department is reported to have said yester-
day that the statement which we published was
'wholly unauthorised'.

In the circumstances, we find it necessary to say
that the statement as printed in the *Irish Times* was
brought to our office on Sunday night by two
members of Dáil Éireann.

No gnat would have survived the unusual welcome

received by the released prisoner in the foyer of a
Dublin hotel. On the landing above stood the Dáil
minister who was also director of organisation and of
intelligence for the IRA. Decorum had no place in this
re-union. With a whoop and a leap Collins cleared the
banisters and landed on the newly-freed Seán. The pair
hadn't had a decent wrestling match since they had last
met in Ballinalee! As he stored away his documented
death sentence, a unique memento which he was to
retain for a lifetime during which it was never officially
revoked, Mac Eoin prepared a statement concerning his
release. It again contained his preoccupation with the
justice of the struggle in which he had participated:

It is now clear that my release by the English
government is an admisson on their part that I am not
only a representative of the people, but a realisation
that the English recognise me as an Officer of the
Irish army. . .
The Irish war was war — waged in accordance with
the prevailing conditions.

Jimmy Mac Eoin's first visit to Dublin city was to
escort his brother home to the bonfire celebrations
awaiting him from Rathowen to Ballinalee;from Colmcille to Drumlish. His sister Lena, who had visited him
regularly in hospital, eagerly looked forward to that
day. At home the excited girl to whom he had written
waited, 'Dear Sister Kathleen: Well my dear little sister
I was agreeably surprised to hear from you,' and he
alluded to her reference about receiving new button
boots. He had promised that on release, 'I will give you
a prize also but it won't be button boots.' The nine-year-
old girl would like a 'prize' but the return of her beloved
brother keeper would be enough.
Harry Boland was on the station platform to see Seán
off, and travelling on the train with him was Alice

Cooney. The pair chatted as the train entered the Mullingar station which brought grim recollections back to the returning hero. Then home and repeated celebrations which the couple attended together. There were banquets and ceremonies, including one presided over by Bishop Hoare at St Mel's College. North Longford Flying Column, whose members had carried on a harassing role in his absence, smiled at their returned leader.

The Blacksmith was back in Ballinalee.

One of his first actions on his return was the setting up of a headquarters in Stafford's Hotel of Longford. Mindful of the importance of the Truce he was prevailed upon to grant an interview to a particular auxiliary who was most anxious to meet him. The man entered Seán's office and gave particulars of his service — five medals, one of them a VC — a forty-eight-year-old veteran of the Great War who knew the Dardanelles better than Clonfin. Seán had spared his life during that action. He had refused to pull the body of a dead comrade from under a tender when ordered to do so because Mac Eoin had called him 'Boy'.

That was why he was there. His mates back in the barracks still ribbed him constantly saying that Mac Eoin didn't think much of him when he called, 'Boy, pull out that dead man: I am going to burn the tender.'

When Seán explained that 'Boy' was not a derogatory term but an irrelevant colloquialism the interviewer expressed relief and sighed, 'I will never understand you Irish.'

A story is told of this period which clearly illustrates Seán's reconciliatory nature. It tells of a distinguished member of the House of Commons who also had connections with a well-known brewery. He went on record as saying that the Irish race should be exterminated. His firm's brew was boycotted in Ireland and some of their kegs were emptied on a Dublin street.

The man had a reason to be bitter. He had lost a son to the North Longford Column. Seán heard that he used to visit the site of his son's shooting every year and he arranged to meet the mourning father on one of his pilgrimages. They talked for hours in an Athlone hotel, according to the story, and became firm friends thereafter.

The first session of the Second Dáil was held at Dublin's Mansion House in August. A private meeting was followed by a packed public session. Collins was accorded a tumultuous welcome on this his first appearance as the architect of a near victory over an age-old enemy. Eamon de Valera too was enthusiastically received. Indeed he was elected president on the proposition of the latest released deputy from Mountjoy representing Westmeath–Longford. Seán Mac Eoin's speech in Irish was drafted by Collins, the president of the Supreme Council of the IRB. Mac Eoin's part in the proceedings appear to be incompatible with his views expressed later on that the IRB and Republic's presidency were one and the same. Following in English, Mac Eoin said,

> You know, and the people of Ireland know, what he has done for Irish freedom. Our hope and our belief now are that he will bring our cause to success. In no generation for more than a century has any Irish leader equalled his achievements. No one has shown himself more fitted to deal with our traditional foe. . . He has been meeting them now as a statesman, and he will beat them as a statesman. The honour and the interests of our nation are alike safe in his hands. . .

General Richard Mulcahy seconded Mac Eoin's proposition and Eamon de Valera became president of the Irish Republic.

Within a few months Seán Mac Eoin was to become a severe critic of his presidential nominee. He felt that De Valera did not join the negotiating delegation for the Treaty because

(a) he was fully aware that he would achieve little more, if not less, than what Lloyd George had already offered him in London and

(b) he hoped that the personable Collins and the adroit Griffith might well negotiate something worthwhile.

And Seán was convinced that they did.

He seconded Arthur Griffith's movement of the motion: *That Dáil Éireann approves of the Treaty between Great Britain and Ireland, signed in London on December 6th 1921.* He believed that the Irish people wanted substance, not shadows. Yet again he reverted to his stand on the legitimate army, saying that as long as it replaced the armed forces of England they could develop their country in their own way. He felt that the Treaty did bring substance from the shadows, that it gave the freedom to achieve progress.

9. Towards Civil War

When the Treaty was finally approved and Arthur Griffith, not without paying tribute to De Valera, assumed the presidency it remained to be seen whether the first native government of seven centuries could, in fact, successfully govern. Unquestionable loyalty from its army is a pre-requisite for any government and despite assurances to the contrary by General Richard Mulchay, Minister for Defence, threadbare patches were already appearing in the thin weave of friendships. Men who had fought together and who had cemented friendships which only the hardship of soldiering can reinforce now found themselves facing each other over a yawning crevasse of conscience. So it was hardly surprising when families became split. Most of the army GHQ staff favoured the Treaty but colourful, competent and charismatic personalities of the struggle for independence opposed it: Joe McKelvey, Liam Pilkington, Liam Mellows, Rory O'Connor, Seán Russell, Ernie O'Malley, Liam Lynch, Oscar Traynor — the list was impressive.

An army convention was demanded by these men but even as it was being postponed Mulcahy was re-structuring his staff, using pro-Treaty officers. The convention eventually took place in spite of Mulcahy finally forbidding it. He had feared its setting up a military junta. Only anti-Treaty officers attended but their message was plain. They would not obey Griffith or his cabinet. They repudiated the Dáil. They had virtually opted for a military dictatorship.

The Irish forces were taking over various barracks and posts from the British. And some posts were in control of anti-Treaty troops.

Only three of Seán Mac Eoin's flying column disapproved of the Treaty. There were more dissenters in the Longford Brigade. He himself strongly supported Griffith, Collins and the Treaty. 'To vacate a position is to lose it,' was his simple reasoning. The British were vacating so they had lost. This was a good beginning from which to work. But 'The Blacksmith' was soon to realise that greater responsibility brought greater problems. He took over Longford Barracks and noted a number of deficiencies. He reported this to his superiors and hurried to undertake the task which gave him great pride, the takeover of Athlone Barracks. Soldiers steeped in British Army tradition waited for the Irish takeover on 28 February 1922. They were impressed by the fine uniformed figure who arrived to discuss procedure with their commander Colonel Hore.

Hore had orders to be out of the barracks by mid-day and he informed Mac Eoin that the hand-over could not possibly be completed in time, it then being eleven o'clock. Seán inquired if Hore considered the inventory to be a true position of stores and equipment. Hore said that he did and Mac Eoin took a pen and proceeded to do what many an officer has regretted doing; he signed for everything in the barracks without checking a single item. Perhaps he was impatient, perhaps excited. He soon found one item deficient. When his troops marched in and he went to raise the tricolour he discovered that the flag-staff had been hacked down and taken away. A local yacht-owner, G.V. Simons, lent a mast so that the ceremony could go ahead. Mac Eoin was in command. Initially his appointment remained that of Officer Commanding the Midland Division comprising Longford, Leitrim and Fermanagh, but he was soon to have the entire Western Command under his leadership.

It is important to reflect on the enormity of the task

being undertaken at this time by Mac Eoin and many like him. A civilian army was taking on a state military role without any code of military law and in a period when the operation of the civil law was virtually suspended. Responsibliity for the protection of life and property rested with the National Army, which had to rely for guidance on the individual experiences and judgement of a number of officers and a gradually evolving system of military procedures. For example, as late as May 1921 the chief-of-staff of the IRA wrote to his director of organisation concerning a report received from the East Connemara Brigade carrying out its first active service operation. He asked to be informed who was the officer in charge of the area then. This was typical of the haphazard system of reporting, making appointments and briefing. A national army had now to be placed on a proper footing.

New uniforms with rank-markings, leather straps and pouches began to appear, first on the Dublin Guards, some on the men who marched into Athlone. Officers wore a green whipcord cap and tunic, cut long in the skirt. Breeches or trousers were of whipcord too and appropriate badges, rank markings and other accessories were attached. Stand collar and patch pockets were common to officers' and other ranks' dress, the latter being made of green serge.

Army ranks of the time were confusing. In ascending order they were: Volunteer, Corporal, Sergeant, Sergeant-Major, Second Lieutanant, First Lieutenant, Captain, Vice-Commandant (Battalion), Lieutenant-Commandant (Brigade), Lieutenant-Commandant (Division), Commandant (Battalion), Commandant (Brigade), Commandant (Division), Brigadier, Colonel-Commandant, Commandant-General (Division), Commandant-General (G.H.Q.), Major-General, General.

The man who had escorted the last British officer out

of Athlone Barracks and past a uniformed guard of honour of Irish soldiers was now the major military figure in the west of Ireland: Commandant General Seán Mac Eoin.

On the famed bridge of Athlone where Sergeant Custume made his name for gallantry the departing British troops met the approaching Irish. The officer in charge of the Irish contingent gave the command 'Eyes Right' to his men and they responded. The salute was not returned by the British.

Those present at the army convention had passed a resolution that the Irish Republican Army should reaffirm its allegiance to the Irish Republic and be controlled by an executive appointed by the convention. This executive of sixteen instructed all anti-Treaty members of the IRA to report to their units even as it announced that the authority of the minister for defence and chief-of-staff would no longer be accepted. Seán Mac Eoin argued that the executive wished to supplant both Provisional Government and Dáil as well as wishing to govern the army. Its troops, occupied certain barracks and posts belonging to the new state and therefore, posed a considerable threat. The new commander of Athlone Barracks was often forced to make trips to Dublin. He was, after all, a politican as well as a soldier. During one of his absences, Colonel Commandant Tony Lawlor was sitting in his office, temporarily in charge, when the local brigade commander, Patrick Morrissey, strode in and announced that he and his men had decided to stand by the Republic. Lawlor told him that they were all doing just that. Tony Lawlor believed firmly in the ceremonial of soldiering — salutes, standing to attention, bearing. He disliked Morrissey's overbearing and insubordinate behaviour. He called a parade of the troops and addressed them in a body. Commenting on their lack of military qualities, he assured them that they would accomplish little if they had in mind a fight for a Republic. Then, to assert his authority, he barked out drill orders and had his men 'square bashing' for a lengthy period before allowing a 'fall out' to stack arms and have a smoke. This was a pre-meditated and clever move. He next ordered the 'fall in' at a spot far away from the arms. He spoke to the men again. And as he spoke their arms were being taken away by another party to the guard room armoury. But the officers still wore side arms. These men were challenged by Tony Lawlor. He told them that if they felt he was bluffing they should call his bluff — but would have to suffer the consequences.

This was the scene which confronted Mac Eoin on his return from GHQ. He adopted a firm line, ordered a parade by companies and spoke to Patrick Morrissey. Their conversation says more about the IRA 'split' than a thousand volumes could. Morrissey said that he was not prepared to obey orders from the government but he was prepared to obey Mac Eoin as his superior officer. The fact that Mac Eoin's authority came from the government made no difference. Seán now clearly realised that what was nominally one army was attempting to serve what was virtually a twin-government state. He threw military niceties to the winds as he realised that an example must be made of the near-mutineers. Before all the men he tore the Sam Browne belt from an officer's back and ordered his ejection from the barracks.

Known sympathisers from the brigade staff received similar treatment. These officers moved quickly and occupied buildings in Athlone, continuing to requisition provisions from the army's contractors in the town. They armed themselves and a band of sympathisers so Mac Eoin was forced to take a chance on the loyalty of the garrison by re-issuing them with the arms taken from them. His gamble paid off and Athlone was cleared without discharging a single shot. Things were not to continue so, however, for all over the country similar situations were arising. The infamous Civil War had, in effect, started.

Twice more the Royal Hotel in Athlone was to be occupied by anti-Treaty forces. Clerical intervention averted nasty situations each time. The hotel garrison eventually surrendered to Mac Eoin, it has been said, in protest against the shooting down of an unarmed pro-Treaty officer, Brigadier General Adamson.

Liam Lynch emerged as chief-of-staff of anti-Treaty forces whose executive, led by Rory O'Connor, consolidated their position. Collins still attempted to put across his message that the Treaty would eventually lead to Irish unity and Mac Eoin often accompanied him on his campaigns. While returning from a meeting in Cork one night an assailant leaped from the shadows to shoot Collins. Seán Mac Eoin waded in and disarmed the would-be assassin. He threatened to shoot him with his own gun but Collins told him to 'let the bastard go'. In Killarney, a platform prepared for Collins' meeting was burned after Mac Eoin and he had brushed aside the local anti-Treaty leader who warned them that the meeting would not be permitted.

These events led to the unanimous passing of a resolution by the Sinn Féin Standing Committee: '. . . it is the earnest hope of the Standing Committee of Sinn Féin that the right of public meeting and free speech will not be interfered with.' Cathal Brugha and Eamon de Valera were among the signatories. Still on the tour with Collins, Mac Eoin's physical toughness again manifested itself in Tralee one evening. Commandant Dinny Galvin had been ordered by him to disarm an anti-Treaty party in the town. He did so and, in addition, took captive those who bore the arms. Mac Eoin did not want prisoners and he abused Galvin for taking them. He was in an ill-humour therefore when the prisoners' leader Humphrey Murphy arrived and demanded the release of his men. He threw Murphy down a stairs, jumped upon him and began pummelling him. Michael Collins heard the commotion and arrived to separate the pair. He locked the seething Seán in a small room and later forced him to come out and apologise to Murphy. Seán often boasted about this demonstration of his strength.

Early in April, Seán Mac Eoin reviewed his situation. His forces held Longford, Athlone and Carrick-on-Shannon. Indeed his brother Jimmy was holding Bally-mahon Barracks. Farther west and north things were less secure. Boyle was firmly in anti-Treaty hands. At a conference held in the famed Bush Hotel and attended by Eoin O'Duffy, Commandant Martin Fallon prop-osed a plan to seize the town. He was given the go-ahead. He did take the town but immediately released all captured anti-Treaty troops. They soon re-occupied Boyle. It was an angry Mac Eoin who threatened to dis-miss Fallon but a humane Seán who acceded to Fallon's request that he be given another chance.

Mac Eoin was worried about diverse arrivals in his area. Some were Munster recruits for the army. Midlanders, of their nature, are suspicious of 'runners' and they take time to accept them. But he was more concerned about fifteen Ulster members of the Royal Irish Constabulary brought as hostages into his com-mand after a raid on Belcoo. After a hopeful meeting in London, Collins was trying to establish a rapport with James Craig. Winston Churchill and other statesmen were encouraging the holding of further meetings and so the imprisonment of the policemen was inopportune. Collins visited the Western Command, ostensibly, a routine inspection tour but in fact searching for the prisoners. Mac Eoin escorted his chief around the area and attempted to hustle him past a tool-shed into which the hostages had been pressed. Here at least he belied the claim of being a 'blind follower' of Collins. He was intent on protecting his own officers who had made the capture.

Still the molesting continued. Railway lines were cut, roads were blocked, shots were fired over the heads of speakers. On 13/14 April, the Four Courts was seized and reinforced as a headquarters for the anti-Treaty executive. Two days later Seán Mac Eoin was to have escorted Arthur Griffith through his command area to address a meeting in Sligo. Anti-Treaty feeling was high in this area and local leader Bill Pilkington, former commandant of the Sligo Brigade, issued a proclamation forbidding Griffith's appearance on the platform. Griffith informed the mayor of Sligo, who had sent him a warning, that he would not succumb to such intimidation. Two days before the meeting the mayor was told by Councillor Seamus Devins that the terms of the proclamation would be enforced. The public were warned not to exacerbate the situation by attending. Anti-Treaty troops seized buildings and prepared firing positions.

National troops under Tony Lawlor and Ned Cooney were rushed to Sligo. They occupied the jail and other locations. It was a drizzling Easter Sunday when a tense city awaited the outcome of what could be the first real show-down in the west. Seán Milroy and Darrell Figgis accompanied Griffith by train. They were met in Longford by the newly promoted officer commanding the Western Command, Major General Seán Mac Eoin, filling an appointment which he reluctantly accepted, fearing he might become bogged down in 'paper work'.

Having reached their destination, Mac Eoin's first action was to stride boldly through the town examining the positions manned by both his own and anti-Treaty troops. He knew that Lieutenant General 'Ginger' O'Connell, deputy chief-of-staff, would be arriving later and he noticed that the hotels ear-marked for their accommodation were occupied by Pilkington's men.

The hostelries, Ramsey's and the Imperial, were visited by O'Connell's men sooner than anticipated. Some were pinned down by fire from within; a few were captured. Seán Mac Eoin raided the Imperial and rescued these — together with a few prisoners. This caused Seamus Devins to parley, asking if some peace formula could be found. Mac Eoin showed his most bumptious *amour-propre* on this occasion and suggested vacation of the post-office and restoration of communications to Dublin as a start. Devins refused; Mac Eoin said there could be no truce. Devins warned that there could be bloodshed and here Mac Eoin displayed great sarcasm as well as ruthlessness. 'There will be buckets of it and it will be the first time Sligo saw any.' He had not been impressed by the War of Independence effort in the area.

Sligo's bellman called out details of the meeting. The sun broke through and an armoured car headed a small cavalcade to the meeting spot. In a pose which would in later years be associated with Field Marshal Rommel, Seán Mac Eoin stood in the leading car, revolver drawn, grim and determined-looking. 'Ginger' O'Connell was on the running-board. Commandants Alec McCabe and Jim Hunt, local War of Independence leaders who supported the Treaty, were among the escorting officers. During his speech, Griffith's tender was guarded by Tony Lawlor (now holding the rank of Commandant-General). In a window opposite stood Ballinalee's Blacksmith, a challenging figure introducing his president and supervising his safety. Arthur Griffith spoke and the meeting went off without incident.

10. Outright War

Mac Eoin had only one stronghold west of the Shannon initially but national forces in Galway began to push east to meet his troops moving west. Up in Donegal Commandant General Sweeney, who had taken Finner Camp on 29 June, also captured posts at Ballyshannon and Bundoran. He was setting out to secure the Inishowen Peninsula. The hold maintained by anti-Treaty forces in the Sligo-Leitrim area, therefore, demanded attention. Michael Dockery held Boyle for the anti-Treaty forces so an attack was launched on their positions there. Mac Eoin sent the armoured car *The Ballinalee* to give support. The tragedy of Civil War became apparent when Dockery, a fine leader of the struggle for independance, was shot dead together with a female bystander.

Boyle taken, *The Ballinalee* pushed on to Sligo. But Mac Eoin knew there would be stubborn resistance even before the city was reached. Accordingly, suspecting a leakage of information among his staff, he issued orders for moving 130 men to Dublin. These he had diverted at Mullingar and detrained south of the town of Collooney. He took personal command of a southern approach while Commandant-General Tony Lawlor moved in from Ballina through Tubbercurry. He was wounded at Ballyconnellan but pushed on to join forces with Mac Eoin despite a number of ambushes. But the support of *The Ballinalee* was missing for anti-Treaty forces had captured it at Dooney Rock. The car's commander Captain Michael Robinson escaped but Commandant Seán Adare and Volunteer Jack Sweeney, who had been sent to remove a felled tree, were killed. Of the troops following in a Crossley tender, Commandant

Paddy Callaghan and Sergeant Jimmy Farrell were killed.

But Mac Eoin had an eighteen-pounder artillery piece, the one used at the Four Courts. He evacuated the town and fired on the anti-Treaty position. He led a bayonet charge on one position. His colleague, Commandant Matt Farrelly, caused one amusing incident in the grim affair when, not uniformed, he stumbled upon a group of anti-Treatyites. 'Quick, follow me,' he called, 'I've been waiting hours for you.' At the double, he led his unsuspecting prisoners up to Mac Eoin. Seán narrowly escaped being shot in Collooney but in fact there were no casualities on either side. He billeted his men in the town and enjoyed some fine salmon, lately prepared by his captives.

Meanwhile, despite surrender demands from Seamus Devins and some flamboyant careering of *The Ballinalee* about the city, Commandant Martin Fallon maintained a precarious hold on Sligo Courthouse for the National Army. The Bishop of Elphin appealed to him to vacate it. Fallon refused and the elderly Dr Coyne remained in the building, no doubt to prevent its being attacked. The redoubtable Alec McCabe, who had led the famed Rockingham raid during the War of Independence, was forced to assume a 'naval command' to counter anti-Treatyites who took to firing from a ferryboat. Mac Eoin returned to Athlone as Tony Lawlor pressed forward into north Sligo.

In an effort to re-unite the forces who had fought the War of Independence, Collins gathered officers from both sides at a meeting on 1 May 1922. Anti-Treaty men like Tom Hales, Florence O'Donoghue, Dan Breen, Humphrey Murphy and S. O'Hegarty signed a document suggesting 'the advisability of a unification of our forces on the basis of the acceptance and utilisation of our present national position in the best interests of

Ireland'.

They suggested:

(a) Acceptance of the fact that the majority of the people were willing to accept the Treaty.

(b) An agreed election with a view to forming a government which would have the confidence of the whole country.

(c) Army unification.

Although Rory O'Connor publicly repudiated the document, Liam Mellows, Seán Moylan and that other anti-Treaty champion Liam Lynch met Eoin O'Duffy, Gearoid O'Sullivan and Seán Mac Eoin only three days later. A four-day truce was agreed to. This lull in hostilities was extended while a committee of ten Dáil deputies, five of each opinion, attempted to 'explore every possibility of arriving at an agreement'. Seán Mac Eoin was a member of the committee which failed to agree and on 16 May separate reports were submitted by each side. Some responsibility for the committee's failure must rest with Mac Eoin who claimed that its terms of reference included acceptance of the Treaty. As Mellows pointed out, both sides had agreed to confer without prejudice to their respective positions.

June was to be an eventful month. It saw the disbandment of the RIC at Mullingar Military Barracks. It brought British Army incursions against border posts. In one of these, Beleek, Mac Eoin stood resolute in defence. Churchill desperately attempted to avert a situation in which Seán might conceivably be killed. The loss of a leading Irish figure at British hands would be most undesirable at this delicate stage. It featured the 'Pact Election' on the sixteenth. This was the first use of proportional representation in the twenty-six counties and aimed at postponing the Treaty issue until a Third Dáil could tease out its implications. Thirty-six Sinn Fein deputies who opposed the Treaty were returned.

Seán Mac Eoin was among the fifty-eight in favour who were elected.

War sounds were heard again but drums, fiddles and flutes were heard a few days later, on 21 June, in Longford. The testing affairs of state were temporarily forgotten as Michael Collins and Arthur Griffith celebrated the marriage of Seán Mac Eoin and Alice Cooney. Father P. Grey married Alice Christine Cooney of Gurteen parish to John McKeon of Clonbroney — Church documentation still adhered to the English forms of names. Eoin O'Duffy of Dublin and Maria Cooney of Gurteen were the witnesses. Among the wedding gifts was one from District Inspector McGrath's mother. On 22 June, as he enjoyed the first day of his Donegal honeymoon, Seán Mac Eoin's fellow-Longfordman Sir Henry Wilson was shot dead in London. On 28 June, the shelling of the Four Courts took place as Seán and Alice were booking into Ramsey's hotel in Sligo. Seán returned to resume command in Athlone.

He had an ADC Captain Louis Connolly and a sergeant driver called Ingram. Anti-Treaty forces withdrew from some of their positions in Sligo that night, apparently under the impression that Mac Eoin's arrival signified a pro-Treaty build up in the area. Mac Eoin took part in fighting the fires and in other actions the following day before returning to Athlone. His wife Alice recalled that journey taking them from 6 p.m. until 3 a.m. due to roads being blocked by trees, diversions and the like. One hold-up took place near Glasson as the tired couple neared the end of their journey, a road block was obviously manned and Seán wanted to get out of the car and shoot it out. His new bride persuaded him to desist. This prevented what could have been a fateful encounter. The barricade had not been put in place by anti-Treaty forces but by men of Seán's own command. In charge of them and ready to fire if the car had not stopped was the officer commanding Bally-mahon Barracks, Commandant Jimmy Mac Eoin, Seán's brother. (Ballymahon is often called, 'the town that is fifteen miles from everywhere'. And 'everywhere' represents Longford, Mostrim, Mullingar and Athlone).

Back dealing with his dreaded paperwork, Seán Mac Eoin began to feel the frustrations of a soldier of the people dealing with a military command structure being established by the Defence Council appointed on 13 July and comprising Michael Collins as commander-in-chief, Richard Mulcahy as minister for defence and chief-of-staff and Eoin O'Duffy as assistant chief-of-staff. Two-way correspondence of the period suggests that Mac Eoin was inclined to resist directions for redistribution of his forces. His reasons were in part humane but mostly astute. The sending of men to the Curragh for training was suggested. Movement of troops in a major reorganisation of his 2,100 strong command was being demanded.

'You should have no redundant men after Saturday 19th (August),' wrote the chief-of-staff.

Seán's reply bore evidence of the problems he faced. He said that he had started carrying out the scheme but 'the first thing I had was six deputations from traders in towns about to be evacuated to leave the garrisons there for their protection'. For their protection or their business interests?

Mac Eoin said that, after consultation with the officers commanding the Third Western and First Midland Divisions, he had decided 'with your consent, to let matters stand as they are for fourteen days.' Quoting the support of Colonel-Commandant Lawlor he then went on to say something which superiors do not like to hear: 'I shall therefore be glad if you can see your way to let the matter stand'.

Mulcahy's reply was reasonably tolerant:

> We are simply going to break up what we have of
> an Army if we leave it any longer in small posts, and
> do not give it proper military training. We are going
> to leave it at the mercy of any small band of irregulars
> with a 'punch' in them. I am sorry that you allowed
> yourself to give in in any way on the point of your re-
> moval, because it opens the way for further represen-
> tations when you come to move them in a few days.
>
> You must see yourself absolutely to have every-
> thing prepared for the systematic putting into opera-
> tion of the scheme on and from the 22nd. I give in to
> you as far as that date in view of the fact that you
> probably have committed yourself to it, but we must
> go straight ahead with our work immediately and
> there should be no further postponement. . . It is
> absolutely necessary to have at our disposal central
> force enough to allow elasticity in our plans.

The 22nd turned out to be a significant date. That
night, returning from an inspection tour of his native
Cork, Michael Collins was shot dead at BéalnaBláth.
When news reached him a shattered Mac Eoin threw
aside yet another memo from his chief-of-staff
complaining about not affording adequate protection to
railway maintenance crews repairing damage done by
anti-Treatyites. He mourned the loss of his commander-
in-chief and close friend. On the following day an
attempt was made to blow up portion of Custume Barracks in which detained anti-Treatyites were held.

Mac Eoin was too shocked by Collins' death to give
the matter much thought. Ten days before he had
mourned Arthur Griffith, another great figure and
another friend but he regarded the Big Fellow's loss as
being 'more tragic than that of Eoghan Roe O'Neill'

who led the Irish to a great victory at Benburb in 1646 and who had kept an army intact despite the chaotic conditions prevailing then. In drawing the analogy had Seán in mind the traditional cause of O'Neill's death at Cloughoughter Castle in Cavan — at the hands of an enemy agent?

Seán felt that Collins' business in Cork which led to his untimely death was concerned with an attempt to persuade IRB followers of Liam Lynch that their place was on the Treaty side.

During the tension following the tragedy a rumour spread rapidly that Mac Eoin himself had been captured in Sligo and was being held as a hostage against reprisals which might follow in the wake of the shooting of Collins. This was totally untrue.

Tony Lawlor continued his relentless campaign in the west. Mac Eoin defended his actions stoutly as he did many others under his command. He wrote strongly worded letters to his chief-of-staff in reply to what seemed to be endless queries—even some concerning anonymous letters undeserving of action by GHQ of an army. He received correspondence back criticising a lack of solid administration or organisation in the west. The Westport–Newport area was giving trouble and it was suggested by Mulcahy that, with the manpower at his disposal, Mac Eoin's results were not gratifying. It was implied that the civilian population in his area of operations were losing confidence in his ability to protect them: 'I cannot help feeling, from odd remarks and various little references to the state of affairs in the west that I hear from time to time, that there is something like this arising in the minds of the people.'

This was in direct contrast to a report submitted by Tony Lawlor which Seán allowed to reach GHQ. The reason must remain a matter of intriguing speculation: out of a devilish sense of humour, as an exercise in egotism or in deliberate impertinent rebuttal? Part of Lawlor's report read: 'To flatter you a little, Sir, but it is the truth, the boys are saying, "Up McKeon and into it".' Mulcahy's annoyance was obvious in his critical reply.

The relationship between Mulcahy and Mac Eoin must remain enigmatic for much of the former's correspondence was formal, often curt and yet it was not uncommon of him to begin 'A Seán, a chara'. As time went on, of course, accepted military methods of reporting became apparent; official army forms came into use — strength returns, statements of posts, equipment schedules.

Gradually anti-Treaty resistance in the west was being overcome. Up around Ballina, Mac Eoin — still staunchly served by Lawlor — was fighting the last stubborn stand of Michael Kilroy and his men while in the Sligo area and across the Ox mountains Liam Pilkington and Seamus Devins were being closed in upon by Seán's own forces from the south and General Joe Sweeney's from the north. *The Ballinalee* was caught in a position which forced its anti-Treaty crew to desert it, taking its machine-gun along.

This episode ended in a tragic action at Ballintrillick on Ben Bulben's broad plateau on 29 September when Seamus Devins, Brian MacNeill, Patrick Carroll and Joseph Banks were shot in an affair about which little is even yet certain. Few incidents of the Civil War aroused such speculation, rumour and bitterness as did the Ben Bulben killings. Brian MacNeill was the son of the prominent minister for education and Treaty supporter Eoin MacNeill, former chairman of the council which formed the Irish Volunteers in 1913 and their chief-of-staff who countermanded Pearse's order for the Easter Rebellion of 1916. A watch was removed from MacNeill's corpse and when MacEoin heard of this some years later he embarked on an investigation to discover the culprit. He succeeded and returned the watch to MacNeill's widow. The fate of the thief is unknown.

Next day the news sheet *Republic of Ireland* screamed allegations that a man who 'drafted the Murder Bill' now mourned his massacred son. It claimed that a curfew was imposed in Sligo on the night of the killings so that the bodies could be secretly brought into the town — there were others besides the Ballintrillick four. Pro-Treaty troops were accused of shooting the victims while they had their hands raised in surrender. 'The Free State 18 pounder blew up their own armoured car, *The Ballinalee*,' it jeered as National reports claimed its being sabotaged by a mine.

Mac Eoin took responsibility for the killing of the armoured car crew and is alleged by some to have said, 'Most of the funerals were ours before that. They were armed and alert and had to suffer the consequences'.

Years of whispered story have spawned sensational, even macabre, averment in connection with what was, in effect, the final engagement in the Sligo area. Mac Eoin found it difficult to understand the attitude of the people of the town and its hinterland: 'They would be with you one day and against you the next.'

There were other encounters within Mac Eoin's command before the Civil War finally ended. Anti-Treaty leader Matthew Davis was captured along with eight others when Quaker Island on Lough Ree was raided. The residence of the late Reverend Sir George Ralph Fetherston, made famous by Oliver Goldsmith's *She Stoops to Conquer*, was fired on 27 February but the caretaker and his family extinguished the blaze. Other arson attempts were made at the Earl of Granard's house, Castleforbes and Clonyn Castle near Killucan — former residence of the Greville Nugent family. In March, National troops on outpost duty at Mullingar railway station were attacked but·there were no injuries.

But the emphasis of action was now on the west: against Michael Kilroy around Newport, whose men vowed to sink the boat that would bring delegates to England to 'complete the Treaty'; against Frank Carty in Foxford; and against John Grealy at Ballyhaunis, with the assistance of Commandant Frank Symons commanding the armoured car *The Big Fellow*.

In January 1923 Sligo railway station was set on fire, causing damage estimated to be £8,000. Railways were prime targets for anti-Treaty forces. A small boy carrying a toy cannon was among those taken off a train at Streamstown, Co Westmeath. The raiders joked with him about the gun as they mined the bridge across which the train had crossed before being halted. The bridge was then blown up and the train pushed back along the rails till it tumbled into the gap created by the mine.

The engineers from Custume Barracks were particularly proud of the speed with which they erected a temporary bridge at Streamstown. They had trains running again within a very short space of time.

Grim tales have been told about conditions in Athlone detention centre where reports claim several hundred were held. Attempts were made to tunnel out of it.

But all tales of the period are not equally serious. Canal barges carrying supplies sent from Dublin to Mac Eoin's Athlone garrison were often raided and the provisions aboard stolen — particularly if they included kegs of porter. Mac Eoin decided to thwart the supposed anti-Treaty acts of inland piracy. He made arrangements for a platoon of national troops to be put on board a barge and disguised as goods covered with a tarpaulin. Sure enough, the raiders struck. Not one anti-Treatyite was captured, however, because they were troops of the national army.

Ammunition and provisions were taken from a train at Kiltoom and Seán sent troops to carry out a search for the missing items. They were found on Inchineena island near Lanesborough. So were nine men of the opposing forces and all were escorted back to Athlone. So it went on — minor and comic incident alike causing a leader irritation. Against all these frustrations and against ever increasing minutes, memos, queries and complaints from headquarters, Seán Mac Eoin orchestrated the death-rattle of the Civil War in the west of Ireland.

11. Soldier and Statesman

The Army would knock the corners off any young lad.
This profound assertion is often heard from people
who admit to a healthy character-formation brought
about by soldiering while never dreaming of partici-
pating in the occupation themselves. In Seán Mac
Eoin's case its sagacity was proven. It rid him of any
sense of inferiority he may have had concerning his rural
upbringing. He realised the need for further study and
so he paid frequent visits to Father Markey for six years
during which time he learned Latin and French as well
as studying English grammar and syntax.

The new responsibilities of self-government rested
lightly on the broad shoulders of Longford's fine son,
not yet in his thirtieth year. A tactful, diplomatic, clear-
sighted and shrewd politician was emerging. Even his
most ardent supporters admit, 'He knew where he was
going and he would do almost anything to light the way.'
His critics say political patronage fuelled the illumin-
ation of his ambitious career and point out the number
of pensions he manipulated for fellow Longfordians —
seventy for the action in which District Inspector
Kelleher was shot, they claim, when seven would have
been a more realistic figure. 'Rubbish,' counter the Mac
Eoin men. 'He looked after people who billeted the
column during the War of Independence. There was no
problem getting pensions for owners of houses compul-
sorily taken over but other means had to be found to
compensate the many kind people who volunteered safe
accommodation to men on the run.'

Long before any pension was set up, however, Mac
Eoin was in need of his people's support. The loyal
allegiance of the officers and men under his military

command was soon to be tested.

When, after the Civil War, the Irish Free State embarked upon parliamentary procedures to place its army on a proper footing an act was passed on 3 August 1923. It made Temporary Provisions in relation to the Defence of Saórstat Éireann, saying:

> Whereas it is provided by Article 46 of the Constitution that the Oireachtas has the exclusive right to regulate the raising and maintaining of such armed forces as are therein referred to. . . It shall be lawful for the Executive Council to raise and maintain an armed force to be called Oglaigh na hEireann (hereinafter called The Forces) consisting of such number of officers and men as may from time to time be provided by the Oireachtas. . .

The operative date was 1 October 1924.

A defence order issued in September 1923, was the harbinger of trouble. The forces had reached the staggering figure of 55,000 and demobilisation was inevitable. The order proposed putting this into effect before 1 April 1924.

There was dissention concerning some of those chosen for retention and about many destined for discharge. This led to what has since become known as *The Army Crisis, The Army Mutiny* or *The Tobin Mutiny*. Its mutinous aspect began when Major General Liam Tobin and Colonel Charles F. Dalton sent an 'Ultimatum' to President William Cosgrave stating that the IRA accepted the Treaty only as a means of achieving its objects, namely the securing and maintenance of a Republic. An order was issued for the arrest of the signatories of the ultimatum and some of their associates. Reaction to this included removal of arms from certain barracks and posts by raids or by absconding troops. Waterford, Baldonnel and Roscommon were mainly affected. The latter, raided on 9 March, was in Mac Eoin's area for his appointment as general officer commanding Western Command had been confirmed on 29 February. Forty-eight rifles, twenty-four bayonets, 3,320 rounds of ammunition, forty bombs and miscellaneous equipment were taken. All but fourteen rifles, twenty-one bayonets, 1,012 rounds and twenty bombs were recovered.

Protest resignations were commonplace. They included Pat McCrea who had participated in Seán's rescue bid in 1921.

On 12 March the Dáil was told by General Mulcahy that everything was normal in the Athlone area. Only two had absconded and there were no resignations. The former were in connection with the Roscommon incident. He assured the house of 'the utmost loyalty of officers and men' in Mac Eoin's command.

Seán remained strangely silent throughout the whole affair. Perhaps his commonsense suggested the danger of statements exacerbating an already explosive situation. Indeed, his sound, unflappable presence assisted the young army right through its early stages. On 18 February 1925 he became GOC Curragh. Realising the urgent need for training and discipline he picked and appointed select legal and training sections.

During 1925 and 1926 Seán's many periods of hospitalisation, resulting from his Mullingar wounds, began in the General Military Hospital at the Curragh. A week in 1925 and two months in 1926 were followed by more frequent and longer treatments during the years ahead.

Then, on 19 March 1927 he was appointed to the general staff as quartermaster general. During that year he went to France as an emissary of the Irish state. He was welcomed by high ranking officers of the French Army from whom he learned about army organisation and military procedures. His words to his hosts proved prophetic: 'Ireland can, and will, remain neutral in the next World War.' On 20 February 1929 Seán Mac Eoin attained the highest position in the army. The Blacksmith of Ballinalee became Lieutanant-General Seán Mac Eoin, chief-of-staff of the defence forces.

After a mere three months in the appointment, however, he decided to retire. He considered that his 'work of organisation was finally done'. Furthermore, the importance of building up an army completely divorced from politics was becoming increasingly apparent and, although he remained on the reserve of officers for a further year, he resigned as chief-of-staff on 10 May 1929.

His wife was later to state that he would have been a happier man had he remained a soldier. Members of his family left in Longford regretted the little time he could spend with them when he became fully embroiled in politics. For the moment, however, he bought a farm at St Anne's Garvagh, not far from Ballinalee, and exercised himself playing an occasional game of tennis. He even set up a small forge where he 'relaxed' on occasions.

12. Political Career

Seán Mac Eoin's entry to the Second Dáil in 1921 as a Sinn Fein deputy has already been noted. The Third Dáil assembled on 9 September 1922 having been prorogued by proclamations issued on 30 June, 13 July, 26 July, 12 August and 26 August. He was still a member. The Constitution of the Free State Act was passed on 25 October 1922 and there was a general election in August 1923. But by this time Seán was involved in the formation of the army of a fledgling state. For him, this took precedence over politics. He was not a member of the Dáil again for about six years. Then William Cosgrave persuaded him to retire from the army in order to contest the by-election in Sligo–Leitrim. He won that seat on 7 June 1929. Winning elections became commonplace. Foreign travel did also.

Earlier trips abroad had included one to Switzerland to solicit support from the Swiss government for Ireland's entry into the League of Nations. In December 1929, the blacksmith who had told Cathal Brugha that he hardly knew his way around Dublin was making headlines abroad. *The Boston Evening American* carried a banner headline:

IRISH GENERAL REVIEWS TROOPS AT BOSTON

Mac Eoin was visiting Lieutenant-General Preston Brown of the First Army Corps, US Army, at South Boston Base. He was building up prestige which was to stand him well at the hustings.

He received 6,249 first preference votes as Cumann na nGaedheal member for Longford–Westmeath constituency in the general election of 16 February 1932. The party won fifty-seven seats to Fianna Fáil's seventy-two,

Labour's seven, Independent Labour's two, Independents' eleven and Farmers' four. That Dáil survived less than a year but the following one remained in office from January 1933 until January 1937. Seán was a member, having polled 7,650 first preference votes for Cumann na nGaedheal. By September 1933, his party had merged with the National Centre Party of Frank MacDermot and the National Guard (Blueshirts) to become the United Ireland Party. Led by Eoin O'Duffy they adopted the title Fine Gael. William Cosgrave, James Dillon and Frank MacDermot were its Vice-Presidents.

Seán was now displaying diplomacy and tact in his political affairs. He was even thanked by Eamon de Valera for his impartiality on one occasion. His success at the polls was strengthening. He topped them against people like M. J. Kennedy and J. Victory — the Sinn Fein judge of his early years — as he fought in the Athlone–Longford constituency.

In the spring of 1939 he spoke on behalf of Ireland at the Inter-parliamentary Union Conference in Oslo where representatives of the parliaments of the world were gathered. His earlier prophecy about Irish neutrality was to be proven correct that year when the Second World War commenced. He was sitting, again representing Athlone—Longford for Fine Gael, in the Twelfth Dáil when he ran for the Presidency. Dr Patrick McCartan ran also against Seán T. Ó Ceallaigh.

Seán's brother Andrew had died a few months before the campaign began. He was a mere forty-seven years of age. This loss was followed by a defeat at the polls which might not have occurred in a two-man battle against Seán T. Ó Ceallaigh. Alluding to this and his later bid for the Presidency Terence de Vere White wrote after Seán's death:

To have been defeated by Mr de Valera in a Presidential Election was not to be complained about. In their earlier relationship the older man was 'The Chief' but he might have expected a deeper place in the hearts of his countrymen than Mr Sean T. O'Kelly who was also victorious at his expense.

The voting was as follows: Ó Ceallaigh—565,165; Mac Eoin—453,425; McCartan—212,834.

In the February 1948 election Fianna Fáil won sixty-eight seats; Fine Gael, thirty-one; Labour, nineteen; Clann na Talmhan, seven; Independents, ten; and the new Clann na Poblachta, ten. A coalition government was formed under Taoiseach John A. Costello. Seán Mac Eoin became Minister for Justice in the cabinet and served in that capacity from 1948 to 1951.

While Minister for Justice General Seán Mac Eoin drew most attention — and criticism — for his blunt refusal to answer questions on the progress of a bill to legalise the adoption of children. His predecessor was alleged to have consulted with the Archbishop of Dublin, Dr McQuaid, on the intricacies of the proposed legislation. Similar allegations have been made against Mac Eoin, supported perhaps by his later jocose reference to the subject: 'I wasn't going to risk a belt of a crozier for anyone!'

It should not be forgotten that Seán was a prominent member of the Knights of St Columbanus, then a secret society formally recognised by the Catholic Church and structured on Masonic lines. Its avowed aim was to foster fraternal charity and develop 'practical Christianity' among its members. Seán was received into Council No 96, Dublin, spent a period with Longford Council and became Provincial Chancellor of Area 1, Dublin for the period 1948-1951. In 1963 honorary life membership was conferred upon him. In 1958 Seán became chairman of the newspaper *The Catholic Standard* and he retained the appointment for a decade.

The Minister's curt dismissal of questions became infuriating to some deputies:

> The examination of the problem is taking longer than I had expected. (December 1948)
> There are certain difficulties which I regret it has not yet been found possible to overcome. (March 1949)

Six further parliamentary questions on the matter remained unanswered. On 29 November 1950 the minister was not in the House when Mr T. F. O'Higgins, minister for defence, replied on his behalf:

> After very careful consideration of this matter I have decided not to introduce proposals for any legislation which would provide for the irrevocable transfer of a parent's rights and duties in respect of a child to any other person.

Seán's attitude reflected the mood of the deputy from the provinces who wryly remarked of the shelved legislation: 'It would be like interfering with the stud-book.' Mac Eoin, however, was still under pressure — even from delegates at his party's Ard Fheis. But he parried saying that no law could be framed which would compel a mother to abandon for all time her rights to her own child.

In his book, *Church and State in Modern Ireland 1923-1970,* J. H. Whyte offered the explanation that Seán Mac Eoin's refusal to answer questions stemmed from his being 'a pious old-fashioned Catholic who found it distasteful to bring the Church into public controversy.'

When, in 1952, the second stage of the Adoption Bill was eventually moved by Mr Gerald Boland, his successor in the Fianna Fáil government, Seán recalled the difficulties with which he had to contend. They were 'mainly of a religious nature,' he said. He was baited

THE SEÁN MAC EOIN STORY

throughout his speech by incessant interruptions from Mr Peadar Cowan. Noticeably impatient, Seán parried all efforts to be drawn on any specific religion he might have had in mind. Yet he himself concluded, 'If the Minister says he is satisfied that he has met with the requirements of the Hierarchy (in that) I am satisfied.'

During the last months of that Dáil's life (March to June 1951) Seán changed from justice to defence. Perhaps it was because of his unhappy experience with the Adoption Bill that he did not figure prominently in the 'Mother and Child Scheme' controversy. The resumption of the earlier 1947 Health Act difficulties occurred later when Dr Noel Browne proffered a formula which would introduce free maternity care for mothers, expectant mothers and children up to the age of sixteen. A Church-State crisis developed. The Irish Medical Association and some of Dr Browne's colleagues opposed the proposals and latched on to arguments from Catholic social doctrine for their own support. They made a direct appeal to the Hierarchy who concurred with their views. The government was requested to drop the scheme. They did. Receiving little support from his cabinet colleagues, Dr Browne resigned his ministry on 11 April 1951. Less than a month later three rural deputies opposed the government which they formerly supported because of its refusal to increase the price of milk. This depleted its majority and Mr John A. Costello dissolved the Dáil.

Dr Browne joined with Independents in support of Fianna Fáil after an inconclusive general election. Mac Eoin headed the poll in Longford–Westmeath for the next two elections, the first of which, in 1954, resulted in the Second Coalition Government taking office. The soldier-statesman was re-appointed to a fitting ministry —Defence.

It was with a sense of pride that he undertook the

various tasks connected with his ministry and during his inspections of barracks and posts he was appreciative of the modern army which had evolved since his own earlier years. A visit to Columb Barracks, Mullingar, gave him particular pleasure and he noted with gratification how the cell in which he had been held after his 1921 arrest was suitably signposted. He was known to halt his car and stop to have a chat with parties of soldiers he might happen upon as they carried out training exercises by some roadside. His interest and enthusiasm was once noted by a young officer who did not know until the day after such an informal meeting that his pleasant visitor was the minister for defence.

In January 1956 Seán saw Ireland's representatives take their seats in the General Assembly of the United Nations for the first time. His thoughts harkened back to his first attempts to have the country represented at the League of Nations. In the same month his brother, Peter, died at fifty years of age. The border campaign of that year disturbed the mourning minister. While visiting Finner Camp in Co Donegal one day for an FCA officers' commissioning ceremony friends of the young newly-commissioned were arriving to a reception. One lady remained outside the camp. Seán was told her reason. She would never 'frequent a Free State Mess'. He spoke quite sharply about her attitude.

He was back topping the poll again in the 1957 general election but the Coalition were defeated when Fianna Fáil won a total of seventy-eight seats.

In December 1958 Seán reviewed Rex Taylor's *Life of Michael Collins* in the *National Observer*. He underlined the important role played by the IRB in the whole revolutionary movement. Again he re-iterated the IRB's claim to being the sovereign government of the Republic, its president being the president of that same Irish Republic. The direction of Cathal Brugha's as minister for defence ordering him to London with twenty-two others in order to wipe out the British cabinet was again commented upon. Mac Eoin used Collins' countermand as an illustration of 'the unique position which Collins exercised in the Government as a result of the IRB'.

Seán also drew attention to the Craig–Collins agreement of March 1922. This signed document committed the Northern Premier to a meeting with the Provisional Government with a view to ascertaining whether means could be devised to secure Irish unity. The Four Courts occupation and the ensuing Civil War nullified the agreement, he wrote, and added that such an agreement would then (1958) be regarded as a major step towards the termination of Partition.

Florence O'Donoghue was in the van of writers to editors disputing Mac Eoin's opinions on the IRB and its presidency. He was to take up the argument again after a television interview between Mac Eoin and Terence de Vere White six years later. The controversy is discussed in Chapter 14.

But meanwhile the Blacksmith of Ballinalee had his sights set on the highest office in the land again. On 4 January 1959 the *Sunday Press* quoted him as saying:

> I would like to mention the fact that when His Excellency, the present President, sought our consent to his nomination by himself of himself for the office of President for a second term, we agreed and the implication was that his opponent who was nearest to him in the 1945 election would be an agreed candidate in 1959.

Far from being an agreed candidate, Seán was pitted against the most formidable opponent Fianna Fáil could muster — Eamon de Valera.

Mac Eoin accused Fianna Fáil of misusing state cars in

1945 when supporting Sean T. Ó Ceallaigh while he and Dr Patrick McCartan had to employ drivers or drive themselves — on an issue of coupons for a ration of 100 gallons of petrol. Later allegations claimed that a million of his election pamphlets were deliberately held up by post office authorities. The latter argued that free mailing didn't apply to presidential election literature but finally lifted the ban.

The election was run in conjunction with a referendum on proportional representation against which Fianna Fáil campaigned. A speech of Seán's made in Longford was typical of the campaign he was running:

> Vote for me, if possible, and vote against the abolition of P.R. but above all vote and exercise the God-given right of the franchise. . .
>
> If that person (elected) happens to be your humble servant, I will retain the principles which have guided me all my life. I will guard those principles and never do to another person what I would not wish him to do to me.

It was a 'man of the people' campaign as was highlighted by another successful deputy who always adopted a similar approach. Oliver Flanagan, T.D., said: 'He is a humble, plain man, one of the people of the country. He is a statesman, scholar, soldier and farmer and he has all the qualities to fill the highest office in the country.'

Even Longford Civil War opponents spoke in favour of Seán but the challange was too great and De Valera won. Seán, however, polled a commendable 417,536 votes to the winner's 538,000. The Irish electorate displayed a sense of discrimination when their vote on the P.R. issue went the opposite way. Fianna Fáil's proposal to abolish the system was trounced.

A politician twice defeated for the presidency might

have been excused for retiring from politics altogether. Not this dogged warrior, however. The Longford–Westmeath constituency provided the headlines during the 1961 election with what became known as 'The Long Count'.

Polling opened on Wednesday 4 October and the count began in Mullingar's County Hall as usual the following morning. Mac Eoin was elected on the fourth count but before the result of the fifth count was announced the Returning Officer, Mr J.D. Ross, adjourned till 3 p.m. on Friday. Seán was leading a Fine Gael protest. It revolved around a group of papers from an Athlone booth. These had been regarded as invalid because of irregularities in their markings. The Sinn Fein Candidate, Rory Brady, received an extra vote as a result, Fine Gail claimed, thus eliminating Patrick Cooney, Fine Gael and nephew-in-law of Seán Mac Eoin. Both had received 2,800 first preference votes and Cooney's elimination was as a result of the disputed vote. Legal wrangling began and the count did not resume until 6 p.m. on Friday and the result became known two hours later. Cooney's elimination was upheld. Although Fianna Fáil's Frank Carter polled more first preference votes, Seán was still the first candidate elected.

The Long Count was over but history was to repeat itself very quickly in the constituency.

13. Defeat

> If ever the history of electoral legislation in this
> country is written the Longford–Westmeath constitu-
> ency will have a chapter to itself. At the 1961 General
> Election it created history in its own right with a dis-
> pute over a ballot paper, and as a result a section was
> written into the 1963 Electoral Act. That was what
> was termed The Long Count. Last week, following
> the casting of the votes in the 1965 General Election
> in Longford–Westmeath, the count began in the
> Temperance Hall, Longford, and did not finish until
> Tuesday last — a real marathon.

So said the *Westmeath Examiner* of 17 April 1965. Mac
Eoin had been regarded as a certainty in the election of
7 April and the first day's count progressed normally.
After the seventh count and a neck-and-neck struggle
preceding it, only thirty votes separated Seán and
Fianna Fáil's P. J. Lenihan. The eighth count ended
with Lenihan seven votes ahead and the returning
officer was about to declare him elected when Mr Denis
Keane of Bunbrosna, Fine Gael's election agent,
demanded a re-count of all votes.

From Friday till Tuesday the re-checking and re-
counting continued. The Temperance Hall was rife with
rumour and speculation: complaints about irregularities
in Mullingar Mental Hospital's voting. Lost postal
votes. Lenihan leading. Mac Eoin leading. Wrong
tallys. Things were serious. Tempers of supporters
became frayed. Garda reinforcements were drafted into
Longford. Magnifying glasses were used to scrutinise
doubtful markings.

On Sunday morning a further re-count was sought on
the grounds that not enough time had been allowed for

proper examination. Another Fine Gael candidate, Mr Paddy Cooney, also looked for a re-check. Both applications were refused and counsel threatened bringing a petition before the High Court. Mr Brannigan, the returning officer, listened to further complaints and pleas but held that if every candidate received the treatment demanded by Fine Gael's counsel there could be a ninety-day count. Eventually Lenihan was declared elected by 6,608 votes to 6,595.

Mac Eoin was a beaten man — in every sense of that word. 'He should never have fought that election; he was a sick man,' said his wife Alice. This was literally true for the general had been removed again to St Bricin's hospital before election day. He was suffering from extreme fatigue and was not allowed visitors. One of the disputed votes in the count bore the message: 'God bless Seán Mac Eoin. May you get well soon.'

His election campaign had begun under a cloud too, for on 27 February his old soldier comrade John 'Bun' McDowell died. The glory of the past was receding for Ballinalee's blacksmith. Some commentators claimed that Seán could not and did not wish to keep pace with the fast development of social changes which emerged during the fifties and sixties. But they reckoned without the mettle that had made Seán the man he was during the twenties and thirties. He was not yet ready to slip away into seclusion.

14. The Sixties

Shortly after a television interview with Brian Farrell on 24 August 1962, Seán favourably received a suggestion from an old opponent in government. It envisaged the formation of a committee of prominent representatives from the War of Independence period. The main object was the establishment of a permanent memorial to commemorate Ireland's patriot dead. People from both sides of the divide created by the Civil War were among those who responded.

The final outcome of this prelude to crossing bridges was Parnell Square's fine Garden of Remberence with its cruciform pond and sculpture by Oisin Kelly depicting the *Children of Lir*. The memorial was designed by Dáithí P. Hanley and was completed in 1966. Before that, however, Ballinalee's famous son was once again to face the daunting new medium, television. This time the outcome was to be less amicable

Early in 1964, Seán was scheduled to meet Terence de Vere White, a distinguished author, member of the Irish Academy of letters, director of the Gate Theatre and Vice-Chairman of the National Gallery in a television interview. For two years this learned figure had been literary editor of the *Irish Times*. Was it an inherent fear of a man of the soil taking on a noted scholar before the whole nation which prompted Seán's thorough preparation for the encounter?

He endured what could almost be described as a rehearsal with Dick Mulcahy. A discussion document began by summing up his basic philosophy about his part in the Irish struggle. It said that when Seán became a Volunteer he undertook to defend the rights and liberties of all the Irish people, irrespective of creed, class or politics. The question of taking up arms was thus decided for him.

The signing of the Covenant by Ulstermen, their setting up of a provisional government and establishment of the Ulster Volunteers (of which there was a full company in Ballinalee) converted him to the view that only by force of arms could freedom be established and defended in Ireland. He felt that Griffith's policy of our own elected representatives establishing their own parliament and abstaining from Westminster was correct and Westminster had not interfered when the Ulster Volunteers took up arms, after all. He and his contempories had the right to establish a Sinn Fein executive and an army executive.

Seán recalled how two officers of the Ulster Volunteers had been executed in Ballinalee, thus finishing the movement there. He stated that if there had been no Rebellion in 1916 there would have been one in 1926 or 1936 — it was inevitable. And it would then have been too late. The Rebellion showed the people of rural Ireland that guerrilla tactics could be successful against the British.

In this discussion document, Seán Mac Eoin alluded to twenty-two lorries being tackled in Ballinalee, not eleven as previously quoted. He was proud of the fact that the 16th Lancers were taken on and they were the only regular troops in the theatre of operations. Other topics were obviously discussed including his being ordered or invited by Cathal Brugha to go to England with twenty-two men to execute government ministers. It was this statement which caused some controversy when the programme eventually went out on 4 February.

Indeed, before it was transmitted at all there were some developments. The interview was recorded and Seán suggested to Terence de Vere White that he should be asked about what Eamon de Valera did in the 'Black and Tan War'. Mr de Vere White did not comply; he felt that Seán wished to say that De Valera was no help at all. If this happened he thought the authorities at the time wouldn't let his answer out on the air. Mac Eoin was cross. He said he shouldn't have submitted to the interview at all and told Terence that he was 'another Frank Mac Dermot'.

Later, however, he was perfectly nice and kind again. The interviewer was convinced that Mac Eoin was temporarily upset at seeing a chance to expose De Valera lost. He later regretted not asking the question. A strange thing happened next. The video-tape of the interview disappeared and there is at least one allegation that it was stolen. It was re-recorded and transmitted. Six days later Seán Mac Eoin met Eamon de Valera at the funeral of the redoubtable Pat McCrea. 'I have a crow to pluck with you some other time,' said De Valera. 'Now's the time to pluck crows,' Mac Eoin replied.

Eamon de Valera began to argue that Collins and Mulcahy had not the authority to annul Cathal Brugha's order. Mac Eoin parried saying it would be a poor state of affairs if the present minister for defence could give an army officer an order other than through proper military authorities.

De Valera also wanted to know if Mac Eoin was referring to him when he made some mention about prejudicing a meeting of the Dáil by holding out on the release of Mac Eoin from prison. Mac Eoin answered a blunt, 'Yes.'

A third item emerged in correspondence to newspaper editors later. Seán Mac Eoin had mentioned a president of the Irish Republic in his interview. De Valera challenged that there was no president of the Irish Republic from 1780 till August 1921 when Mac

Eoin himself proposed De Valera for the office. 'Nonsense,' said Mac Eoin, laughing heartily. He pointed out that Henry Moore was president of the Irish Republic of Connaught in 1798. Furthermore, under the constitution of the Irish Republican Brotherhood, the president of that movement's Supreme Council was president of the Irish Republic.

Soon the newspapers latched on to one or other aspect of the interview for editorial comment while the 'Letters to the Editor' pages bulged with observation. Some related to details about his release at the time of the Truce but the majority quarrelled with his interpretation of the presidency, just as De Valera had done.

Florence O'Donoghue took up the argument he had begun in 1959. He explained that Collins by virtue of his position as president of the Supreme Council of the IRB *could* and *did* countermand the orders and flout the authority of the chief-of-staff and minister for defence, thereby defying and over-riding the constitutional authority of Dáil Éireann. Collins he maintainted was acting in contravention of an amendment to the Constitution of the Supreme Council of the IRB. That amendment was made in September 1919 and its effect was to delete from the Constitution the claim that the IRB's president was in fact president of the Irish Republic. It also aimed at bringing IRB members under the authority of Dáil Éireann. O'Donoghue admitted that, prior to September 1919, Clause 22 of the Constitution read:

> The President of the Irish Republican Brotherhood is in fact as well by right President of the Irish Republic. He shall direct the workings of the IRB subject to the control of the Supreme Council or Executive thereof.

The amendant to the clause stated that:

The President of the Irish Republican Brotherhood shall direct the working of the IRB subject to
the control of the Supreme Council or Executive
thereof.

It was reasoned for thus:

In view of the fact that IRB policy had succeeded in
establishing a duly elected public authority competent to declare the will and give expression to the
desire of the Irish people to secure international
recognition of the Irish Republic and whereas this
public authority has declared that all servants and
soldiers of the Irish Republic shall take the following
oath:

*I, A.B., do solemnly swear (or affirm) that I do not
and shall not yield a voluntary support to any pre-
tended Government, authority or power within
Ireland hostile and inimical thereto, and I do further
swear (or affirm) that to the best of my knowledge and
ability I will support and defend the Irish Republic and
the Government of the Irish Republic, which is Dáil
Éireann, against all enemies, foreign and domestic,
and I will bear true faith and allegience to the same,
and that I take this obligation freely without any
mental reservation or purpose of evasion, so help me
God.*

It is decreed that members of the IRB may, in accordance with the terms and spirit of their inception oath,
loyally accept and obey this authority.

It is interesting to note that Michael Collins became
acting president of the Republic in 1920 due to Eamon
de Valera being in the USA and Arthur Griffith and
Eoin MacNeill under arrest. Alluding to this incident,
Dorothy MacArdle pointed out that Griffith might have
been expected to nominate Cathal Brugha as his successor, 'but Michael Collins was head of the IRB.' Accord-

ing to Fenian tradition, she stressed, the head of the brotherhood was the real head of the whole movement and of the revoluntionary government and so Collins 'was merely succeeding, officially, to the position which was already accorded him secretly by the IRB.'

Seán Ó Maolain continued the correspondence by posing the question: If Michael Collins was president of the Republic then why did Seán Mac Eoin himself, on 26 August 1921, place before the Dáil, the National Assembly in public session, the proposition that Eamon de Valera be elected as president of the Irish Republic. He pointed out too that Richard Mulcahy seconded the proposition. Both these men were members of the IRB. Furthermore, De Valera was elected without opposition in a Dáil comprising deputies many of whom, including Collins himself, were members of the IRB.

Seán Mac Eoin's conviction about IRB presidency going hand in hand with presidency of the Republic was steadfast. He went further than regarding the office as being then merely symbolic. He felt that, even if dissolution of the IRB could be proved, its members would be bound by former responsibilities and by the oath of the organisation.

His adherence to this principle prevented him from publishing his autobiography in later years. The IRB oath of secrecy was uppermost in his mind when he told Desmond Rushe of the *Irish Independent:* 'When I am dead and gone I am a free man but I am still bound by the oath. I have to put it down in black and white but I feel I have to leave it there.'

Mr Rushe's article appeared in June 1968. Seán Mac Eoin wrote a chastisement to the newspaper. Desmond Rushe had spelt his name Mc Keown. Seán pointed out that his name, as written in his birth certificate, was Mc Keon and he was so described in the British charge-sheet for his court martial in 1921. Furthermore, he had used the Irish form of his name, Mac Eoin, since 1904. Spelling of the patriot's name has always been erroneous. Another Lieutenant-General Seán Mac Eoin who distinguished himself by being appointed chief-of-staff of the defence forces at home and Supreme Commander of the United Nations Forces in the Congo, used the English form *Mc Keown*. Both men have appeared under the same entry in some book indices. There are seventeen variants and synonyms of *Mac Keown,* the main sept of which hailed from Connaught. The *Mac Keons* were of Scottish descent and their main sept was located in Antrim's glens. While both Irish forms of spelling were similar, therefore, there was a vast difference in ancestry between the two men.

The regard in which Seán was held, even by those who opposed him politically, was underlined as late as 1970 when he returned to his native Longford for a meeting of the Clonfin Memorial Committee, held in McElvaney's of Coolarty. There present were men, members of the old column, who often had been critical of his actions, who had sometimes received rebuffs which hurt their pride. Some of them had found it difficult to appreciate that a leader was not always in a position to divulge every detail of a proposed action to his men. Seán was a discreet man and this attribute had often been confused with aloofness.

Supporter and critic alike, however, awaited the arrival of their chief with excitement — and left an armchair in the place of honour by the fire. He entered and accepted the seat. This was his right. All approved and acknowledged the fact. He was gracious, not arrogant, in adopting the role of leader again.

'I'm glad to see you anyway, Seán,' one man said. An amount of water had run under the bridge since they had fought together in the column. Their ways had taken that sad parting when Civil War shattered their dreams.

And the word 'anyway' credited the speaker as much as it did the addressee. In spite of all that had occurred the bond which binds soldiers had surmounted all feelings of rancour. The commanding officer was back among his men and they *were* glad to see him.

15. Last Days

In April 1972 Seán Mac Eoin was yet again admitted to St Bricin's Military Hospital. Fellow patients told how he loved to reminisce, how he spoke respectfully about people. Colonel John Kane remembered how he always spoke of Mr de Valera — never Dev or any other abbreviation.

He boasted a little. How he had once pulled the pin from a grenade and threatened anti-Treaty troops who surrounded him that they would 'all go up' if he were not released. He displayed an unquestioning respect for the clergy and obedience in any matters which could be regarded as bordering on their territory.

He insisted on giving officers their appropriate rank and addressing them by it. He still impressed new acquaintances as a man with a clear, well-ordered intellect, a man of propriety, who was courteous, convivial and capable of transmitting a cheerful confidence.

Reminiscing about his part in the struggle for independence, he bore out Emmet Dalton's observation that he 'brought a glimmer of decency into a dark and sordid era'. While he admitted to being tough, often ruthless (he described himself as acting like a young savage on occasions), he stood firmly by his conviction that he observed the conventional usages of war.

He expressed disagreement with the idea of hunger strikes. Here again his religious beliefs motivated his reasoning. He considered the weapon to be suicidal and therefore sinful. Seán loved to argue the case for the Treaty insisting that the opening of Treaty negotiations between Britain and Ireland was the first step in the abolition of the British Empire. There was no doubt in his mind that Irish unity would have emerged from it but for the Civil War. He stoutly proclaimed that the death of Collins deprived Ireland of a man capable of leading her out of her Calvary to a great new resurrection, a man who would have become a major world figure.

Seán's hospital conversations embraced a colourful life-span. One of his proud boasts was his reception in private audience by two Popes, Pius XI and Pius XII. He liked to point out that he was a member of the Royal Dublin Society and of two golf-clubs — Newlands and Longford.

The leader from the troubled past who had such a distinguished career gave an unexpected answer to a friend who asked him what was the proudest moment of his eventful life. Seán didn't have to think. He had no doubt. It was that day back in his youth when his industry after his father's death enabled him to buy a home for his mother and family.

Of a sentimental nature, he had called his Dublin home in Stillorgan after the townsland of his youth, although he spelt it slightly differently — *Cloncoose*. Mounted on display in his living-room was a fine pipe. On the day before his wedding Michael Collins had given his aide, Bill McKenna a pound note and told him to go and buy the best pipe in Purcell's as a gift for Seán. Bill recalled that the most expensive pipe in the shop cost a mere twelve and sixpence.

But the time for reminiscing was running out for Seán's condition was deteriorating. A noble life was ebbing away, finally succumbing to the effects of that bullet received in a dark Mullingar lane back in 1921.

General Seán Mac Eoin died at St Bricin's Hospital on 7 July 1973. Obituaries were generous in his praise:

. . . the last of the redoubtable figures of the IRB. Not from him was enmity ever shown towards families who grew up in a different tradition. . .

. . . It is accepted that command springs from leadership and that leadership depends primarily on personality, knowledge and example. There is no doubt that Seán Mac Eoin possessed those qualities and must provide inspiration and respect in those who follow. . .

. . . In politics he showed the same steadfast courage and cheerfulness in victory and defeat. . .

It is extremely difficult to describe General Seán Mac Eoin in terms that younger people will understand, because he embodied a virtue which I suspect has completely disappeared from the modern world — Chivalry. . .

These are excerpts from the journal of his beloved defence forces, *An Cosantoir,* written by General Seán Collins Powell, and from a former political leader, James A. Dillon. His television interviewer, Terence de Vere White, wrote in the *Irish Times:* 'Ideally he should have been unconnected with parliamentary politics. . . He was a Cincinnatus who in time of emergency would have come at the peoples' call from his farm.'

He was also referred to as 'one of the most famous individual fighters in the War of Independence'.

The Sunday Press commented: '. . . as leader of this (North Longford) column, Mac Eoin's name passed into legend as the hero of the famous Ballinalee ambush.'

An Taoiseach Liam Cosgrave said, in a telegram to Seán's wife Alice: 'His outstanding qualities will always be remembered and his exploits will be recalled with admiration.'

In its editorial of 9 July, The *Irish Independent* said:

With the death of General Seán Mac Eoin, the legendary Blacksmith of Ballinalee and close friend of Michael Collins, there passes a figure who has been at the centre of a legend of bravery and gallantry during the past fifty years and more.

We admit that accounts of past exploits lose nothing in the telling, that the noble become impossibly noble and the ignoble impossibly evil, but allowing for these overlays no one denies that Seán Mac Eoin was a man of outstanding calibre and nobility who inspired devotion among his friends and great respect among his enemies. . .

. . . his adherence to the highest codes of military chivalry are as relevant an example today in this country as they were in the twenties. . .

Weak sunshine picked out the brass of a soldier's button or slid across a slated roof in Ballinalee. Groups of people huddled outside its Church of the Holy Trinity. They had been unable to gain admission for every major figure in the state was packed inside. Crackling over the public address system came the homily delivered by Dr Cahal B. Daly, Bishop of Ardagh and Clonmacnois:

Wherever green is worn, indeed wherever men cherish freedom, or the oppressed struggle to be free, the name of General Seán Mac Eoin will be remembered in honour, with pride and with affection.

He was among Ireland's bravest and noblest fighters for freedom. He is remembered for a courage that is rightly legendary. But he is remembered even more for a chivalry that is rare in the annals of wars of liberation, a chivalry which, at risk of his own life, refused again and again to leave the field of battle till the wounded enemy was assured of medical care or the dying enemy given the supreme charity of spiritual assistance. General Mac Eoin the soldier never deviated from the call of the Easter Proclamation that 'no one who serves (the Irish Republic) will dishonour it by cowardice, inhumanity of rapine'. By his 'valour and discipline' he proved 'worthy of the august destiny' to which the leaders of 1916 summoned the Irish nation.

But Seán Mac Eoin is remembered inseparably as a man of deep Christian faith and piety and unfailing daily prayer; a man whom no risk or threat would deter from Sunday Mass; a leader who led his men in prayer as resolutely as he led them in combat; a man for whom the Rosary was a natural part of daily living, and who waited for death rosary in hand, in the sure hope that, in the words of Blathmac, the eighth-century Irish poet, 'beautiful Mary, sun of women' would make 'a welcome for him into the eternal, ever-enduring kingdom'.

Seán Mac Eoin will be remembered in Irish history as a man of peace and reconstruction and reconciliation. It was perhaps peculiarly the art of the blacksmith of Ballinalee to turn the sword into a plough share. Mac Eoin gave the best of himself and the best part of his life to tasks of peace, the tasks of giving political structures to freedom and making the structures work. It has been suggested that the successive founders of our modern state were 'politicians by accident', even reluctant politicians. I think it would be truer to say that they were reluctant soldiers, happier in the constructive work of politics than in the grim business of war.

Men still speak today of completing the unfinished business of the men of 1916-1922. There is, after fifty years, much unfinished business still to do for Ireland. But the weapons of its completion are no longer rifles and grenades. Violence is not only irrelevant to the Irish nation's 'august destiny' in 1973; it puts in gravest peril all that has been acheived; it sets back by decades, perhaps by generations, all that is still hoped for. The tools of Irish patriotism now are not the weapons of war but the politics and economics of social justice and the structures of inter-community peace. The unfinished business of 1916-1922 can even today find no better formulation than the words of the Democratic Programme of the first Dáil Éireann:

We declare that we desire our country to be ruled in accordance with the principles of Liberty, Equality and Justice for all, which alone can secure permanance of government in the willing adhesion of the people.

We affirm the duty of every man and woman to give allegiance and service to the common wealth, and declare that it is the duty of the nation to assure that every citizen shall have the opportunity to spend his or her strength and faculties in the service of the people. In return for willing service, we, in the name of the Republic, declare the right of every citizen to an adequate share of the produce of the nation's labour.

The legitimate successors of the patriots of fifty years ago, the authentic heirs of the brave men of Longford who fought at Ballinalee and Granard, are those who work, in unqualified commitment to non-violence, that the ideal of freedom, equality and justice become more and more the reality of the Ireland of tomorrow. . .

May General Mac Eoin's soul, with the souls of all who served Ireland in war and in peace, rest in eternal peace.

Go ndeannai Dia trocaire ar a anam.

In St Emer's churchyard a few hundred yards away a grave had been opened at the back wall to the left of the main path. The grave of another member of the North Longford Flying Column, John McDowell, was to the right of the gaping hole. Across the path was another grave — Paddy Mullally's, a neighbour who had lived near the cottage of Nannie Martin where Seán had the shootout. A friend. A plain countryman uninvolved in any movement.

As the Mass ended a driver from Mullingar Army Barracks quietly started the engine of his vehicle which would tow the gun-carriage bearing the remains.

Survivors of Longford Brigade wearing their medals led the cortège from the church. An army escort flanked the tricolour-draped casket. The Athlone-based Band of the Western Command, with muffed drums, struck up the Dead March and preceded the crowd along the narrow road up towards the Protestant church. That church, Ballinalee, Athlone, Mullingar, Longford — each location had a significant connection with the turbulent years of his gallant youth.

Only a few of those who had come to pay tribute could cram into the cemetery.

They had done as he had requested. The Blacksmith had been laid to rest 'between the "Bun" and Mullally'.

Appendix

Of the many ballads sung about the Blacksmith of Ballinalee, the following is part of a little known one offered to me by Lieutenant Colonel Seán Clancy.

'You stand charged with murder,'
The judge sternly said.
'No, I fought for my country,
For her sake I bled
For Ireland's fair honour.
Your charge I disown
And I'll die for Old Ireland,'
Said Commandant Mac Eoin.

'When your troops I captured,
I treated them right
As persons of war
Who had lost in the fight.
For myself all I ask
As a soldier to die,
That my body at home
With my comrades may lie.'

Then away to the prison
This hero was borne.
Perhaps to die on the scaffold
On a bright Summer's morn.
But the fates in their courses
Had taken a hand,
For a truce is declared
All over the land.

Said England,
'I'll let all your deputies go free.
That all of them meet
And make terms with me,
But there's one man I'll hold
And there's one man alone
And that man is known
As Commandant Mac Eoin.'

But the great Michael Collins
Said, 'This will not do,
If you keep Seán Mac Eoin
Your words are not true.
If a truce is to hold
And if peace is to be
We demand that at once
Seán Mac Eoin is set free.'

For a while England hedged
As often of yore.
But then showed she'd more sense
Then ever before.
The gaol gates are opened,
Mac Eoin is set free.
When the conference opens
With his comrades he'll be.

Then long may he reign
To fight the old cause
Till Ireland again has
Her own freedom and laws.
For I'm confident now
We'll soon have our own
Then long life and glad luck
To Commandant Mac Eoin.

123

Index

124

Who's Who in the Irish War of Independence 1916-1921
Padraic O'Farrell

Who's Who in the Irish War of Independence 1916-1921
examines this generative period in Irish history. It deals
with the personalities involved in both sides of the
struggle and, in a compilation of over 1,000 pen
pictures, lists not only the main activists but many other
combatants who played supporting but equally
important roles in the conflict.

The author's researches covered both public and
private sources and he has had access to previously
unavailable material. His examinations have included
archives, records and journals of the Royal Irish Constabulary, Dublin Metropolitan Police, Royal Ulster
Constabulary, Irish Defence Forces and the British
Army. In the appendices he gives a chronology of the
main events and lists the dead on both sides. The result
is a comprehensive and objective survey of the Irish
fight for Independence.

Hardbound £9